WRITE
your own
MYTHS

STERLING CHILDREN'S BOOKS
New York

An Imprint of Sterling Publishing Co., Inc.
122 Fifth Avenue
New York, NY 10011

First Sterling edition published in 2021.

ISBN 978-1-4549-4178-1

Distributed in Canada by
Sterling Publishing Co., Inc.
c/o Canadian Manda Group,
664 Annette Street, Toronto,
Ontario M6S 2C8, Canada

For information about custom editions, special sales,
and premium and corporate purchases, please contact
Sterling Special Sales at 800-805-5489 or
specialsales@sterlingpublishing.com.

Manufactured in China

2 4 6 8 10 9 7 5 3 1
02/21

sterlingpublishing.com

WRITE
your own
MYTHS

Your Guide to Writing the Most Legendary Stories

Philip Womack

Illustrated by
Anette Pirso

STERLING CHILDREN'S BOOKS
New York

CONTENTS

ABOUT THIS BOOK

In this book you'll find eight chapters, each concerning a particular aspect of creative writing, from BEGINNINGS through to—well, you guessed it—ENDINGS.

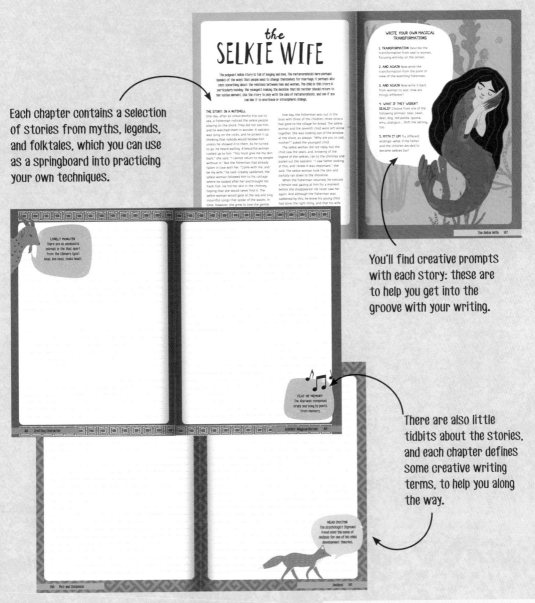

Each chapter contains a selection of stories from myths, legends, and folktales, which you can use as a springboard into practicing your own techniques.

You'll find creative prompts with each story: these are to help you get into the groove with your writing.

There are also little tidbits about the stories, and each chapter defines some creative writing terms, to help you along the way.

MEET PHILIP

Writing, and the joy and skill of writing (as well as its more difficult parts), are immensely important to me, and I'm thrilled to be producing this book for you to test out and have fun with your own.

I like to write, when I can, with a pen and paper. This isn't always possible (especially when deadlines loom). Drafting your work by hand, away from a computer screen and all its distractions, is a really useful exercise. Your brain and your hand are intimately connected, all flowing in a gorgeous, unbroken line.

I hope that you'll find plenty of stories here that will inspire you to scribble down your thoughts, to form them into stories, to explore and enjoy. Each one here will lead you off down many paths.

Good luck!

THE INSPIRATION BEHIND MY BOOKS:

The Other Book, my first novel, was inspired by the legend of Merlin and Vivien. Vivien was an enchantress who coveted Merlin's power; she tricked the old man into handing over his magic before imprisoning him for eternity. It made me wonder: What if they had a child? Would it be their job to guard their magic?

The Liberators, my second novel, was inspired by a picture of the god Bacchus, by Titian, which hangs in the National Gallery, London. He's followed by his Maenads, and he's about to rescue Ariadne, who's been abandoned by the hero Theseus. In my novel, the god's staff was being used by a pair of villains who wanted to create chaos in London.

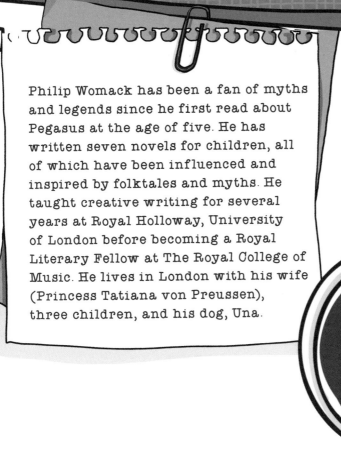

Philip Womack has been a fan of myths and legends since he first read about Pegasus at the age of five. He has written seven novels for children, all of which have been influenced and inspired by folktales and myths. He taught creative writing for several years at Royal Holloway, University of London before becoming a Royal Literary Fellow at The Royal College of Music. He lives in London with his wife (Princess Tatiana von Preussen), three children, and his dog, Una.

The Darkening Path series (The Broken King, The King's Shadow, and The King's Revenge) is based on the fairy story of Childe Roland (like Alan Garner's Elidor). In the tale, Childe Roland is playing with his little sister, when they throw a ball over a church. His sister, Burd Ellen, goes to retrieve it—by walking around the church counterclockwise. She vanishes from sight: she's been snatched away by the King of Elfland, and Roland must enter into a quest to find her. In my version, a young boy called Simon wishes for his little sister to vanish and is surprised when she actually does disappear, taken away to a different dimension.

The Double Axe, reimagined the story of the Minotaur from the perspective of one of the children of King Minos. And that led me to thinking about the ancient world in general and what happened to all those heroes who returned from their travels and settled down and had children. This became inspiration for my next book.

INTRODUCTION

When I started rereading and researching the stories that make up this creative writing book, I was struck once more by the vast array of similarities across folklore, myth, and legend. (Incidentally, I've chosen stories from the rich legacy of folklore and legends, such as those of King Arthur and Robin Hood, as well as from ancient classical mythology.)

Tests, magical objects, heroes and heroines, visits to the *Underworld*—all over the world, you'll find something recognizable in a local story. The Northern trickster Loki has his counterpart in an African hare. Both Psyche in Italy and Vasilisa in Russia must sort through piles of beans with animal help to outsmart an angry goddess. Across the centuries, in desert hammocks, ice-bound igloos, walled gardens in China, and Edwardian nurseries in London, children (and adults) have thrilled and gasped at the same stories.

There are hundreds of connections, even in the small collection of tales I've chosen here. (This has been the subject of much study, which you can look into if you're interested: check out Vladimir Propp and his analysis of folktales.) Their plots are brisk and vital; characters are (usually) either good or evil; and there isn't much room for background or character development.

DIG INTO THE STORY

That is where you, dear reader-writer, come in. This rich store is there for you to delve into, rummage through, revel in, and use to help with your own writing. Legends and myths are a treasure chest, a tapestry, a diamond mine. Delve, dig, discover, and use.

Story is as much a part of what makes us human as our voices or our fingers or our liking for extra cream on our strawberries. Following exciting, surprising plots; empathizing with protagonists; hating villains; enjoying and marveling at landscapes and incidents: all of these are central to the way that we experience the world.

Once you're hooked on story (well, the reason you're here, probably, is that you already are), you very often develop an urge to make your own.

In this book, you'll find some summaries of myths, fairy tales, and legends, drawn from all over the world, and alongside them, plenty of fun and playful tips and prompts to get you writing. You'll look at myths from different angles, learn about the basic building blocks of writing stories, and test your own capacity for imagination. The most important thing to remember is that this is fun: nobody's testing you, nobody's marking you. You can stretch out and enjoy your writing, trying out voices, styles, and moods.

GET INTO THE WRITING HABIT

All writers develop their own routines. Some are happy writing 1,000 words a day; others 300; some can stretch to 5,000. Some plan with minute attention to detail; others have a sense of a general shape, and fill in as they go. Still others simply write to see what happens to the characters that have formed so perfectly in their minds. Some build their fictional worlds to the last tree, the last doorknob, the last biographical detail of the last minor character; others are happy seeing where they go and build up worlds as they write. We all have strengths and weaknesses, and part of the joy (and difficulty) of writing is learning how to overcome them.

All of my books have been written (developed, constructed) in different ways. I've planned them finely; I've zoomed through, being led by characters; I've started

at the end, I've gotten stuck in the middle, I've drafted and redrafted and discarded and redrafted. As you read and learn and practice, you'll find some methods suit you more than others, but you'll always see that there's no one way to do something. You can always improve. Every time you write, you will learn something new about yourself and how you write.

There are lots of tricks that can help you to get writing. I am a great believer in silence, in thoughtful reflection, and in the pen on the page (rather than the finger on the keyboard). Drafting something with a pen means that only you and the writing are connected: you can't check your email at the same time, or text a friend. It frees your mind, and when your mind is free, it makes connections in unusual and interesting ways.

We are bombarded with texts, emails, images, noise, music. You may be messaging a friend at the same time you're watching a TV show on your laptop. You may be listening to something on your headphones while you research something else on the Internet. You may be busily liking your friends' social media feeds and posting your own.

My advice is: close it all down. Choose somewhere quiet. Grab a notebook—or this book. Find a pen. (You'll discover pens you like, pens you don't.) Close your eyes and clear your mind, and then scribble down whatever comes into your head for ten minutes. You can use word lists, maps, plans. Hoard ideas, images, sentences, thoughts. Scraps of material can become the basis for something much, much bigger. Keep those notes, and refer back to them. They may surprise you in time. From those scraps, you'll be able to construct a story. Always think about form: what are you writing, and why? Think about structure: in what order are you telling the story, and why?

One thing to remember about writing is that you may feel very close to what you've written. That beautiful word you've chosen. That pleasing image you've put down. "It is my baby!" you cry. "Don't be cruel!" But that pleasing image, once

you've read it again, may turn out to be not so pleasing. That beautiful word may be doing the opposite of what you think it is.

One of the mistakes new writers make can be thinking that writing all comes in a great, creative rush. We sit, goes the legend, at our computers, tapping out pages (which we then immediately send to our editors). Our writing sits, perfect and unalterable on the page. Popular culture has a lot to answer for in this regard: it's much more compelling to show a writer pouring her heart out by candlelight than it is to show her writing one line, then scratching it out and starting again. If you can understand the writing process—that it can be a stop-and-start thing as well as a rush—then that's a great beginning.

STEP AWAY FROM THE PAGE!

All writers need to step away from their writing and see it from another perspective—that of the imagined reader. This is the crucial part of writing anything, from an essay to a short story to a poem to a novel. You must be able to imagine someone else reading it: you need to see your audience. (Hello, audience!)

If you can learn to take critiques, and rewrite your work until it sings and sings, then you'll be happily on your way. Read out your work—to yourself, into your phone, into the mirror, to your friends and family (as much as they'll let you). Listen to yourself, and listen to your friends. Then redraft. Swap your work with other friends, and read theirs: make notes on it. Think about how the story's flowing, what words they're using, whether things make sense... and then apply those things to yourself.

The prompts that follow are simply that— prompts. They're meant to galvanize you, encourage you, guide you. You don't have to use them exactly as they are: they're starting points, setting you off on a journey into the wonders of fiction. You can twist them and mix them up as much as you like.

Sometimes, the best things happen when you're not trying to make them happen. Read the tales in the following pages, and spark new ones. Take the sword away from King Arthur and give it to Guinevere. Turn Medusa into a man. Give him eels instead of snakes. Give a unicorn wings, make the kraken crawl on land, do whatever you like. Write your own myths.

CHAPTER ONE
GETTING THINGS GOING

Myths and folktales are supremely efficient storytelling machines. They gleam and purr, like a perfectly constructed engine. There's no fuss, no dilly dallying. They get going, galloping into the plot, shoving their heroes and heroines into their quests to slay the dragon, find the magic potion, or do whatever it takes to save the world. You can learn gallons, oodles, gazillions of useful things from their storytelling methods. Once upon a time, one or two sentences, and you're in.

It's almost like magic. Some people think that (some) folktales are memories of magical and shamanic rituals: it certainly feels like you're under a spell when you're in their grip.

As a writer, how can you make sure that your stories start in the right place? How do you grab readers, immerse them in your fictional world, and haul them along, if not kicking and screaming (we wouldn't want that, would we), then at least utterly hooked, all the way to the end?

Many writers struggle with beginnings. Trying to choose where to start can feel like chopping off a snaky head from the mythical Hydra, as two

more spring up in its place. You've got (literally) a whole world of possibilities at your command. But where, exactly, do you start? And, perhaps more importantly, why do you start in this particular place?

The Roman poet Catullus wrote a long poem, which tries to pinpoint where the Greek myths began. He started with the hero Peleus sailing on the *Argo* and his first sight of the sea nymph Thetis. "Why there?" I hear you ask. Because Peleus marries Thetis, and it's at their wedding that the goddess Eris, or Strife, hurls the golden apple that starts the Trojan War.

ESSENTIAL ELEMENTS

First, work out the essential elements of your story. We'll have a look at that in more detail later when we talk about plot (see page 118). Then identify the prime mover: the event that kick-starts the whole shebang. The starter's gun, if you like, or the match that sets the flame.

You'll find you have many options, but you can test each of them. Remember that trial and error, experiment and failure, are crucial components of becoming a writer.

I've chosen the cycle of legends that flourished around King Arthur, because they are an excellent place to, well, start thinking about the start of things. They are stuffed with events: wars, murders, adultery, strange beasts, quests, green giants. You can imagine the early poets and storytellers scratching their heads in puzzlement when it came to identifying the beginning. "Sirrah," one would say to another over a grail of wine. "Should I start with the story of Queen Ygraine, the mother of Arthur?" "Nay, my lady," comes the reply. "I will begin with the wizard Merlin..." This is exactly why myths and legends are so compelling: because their material provides so many possible openings.

Most tellings of the Arthurian stories

commence with the birth of the Big Cheese himself. He was an illegitimate son of King Uther Pendragon and Queen Ygraine of Cornwall, whose husband was at war with Uther. Arthur was then concealed, for his own safety, by the wizard Merlin in the castle of Sir Ector, until the time should come for him to become king.

Could an even more compelling beginning take place further into the story? When Arthur, Ector, and Ector's son, Kay, travel to London when Uther Pendragon dies, and Arthur sees an innocuous-looking sword poking up out of a stone in a churchyard, he picks it up with ease, and the rest is history. Well, legend at least.

The beginning needs to tell us what kind of story we're in: what genre, what style, what voice. (There are many genres: crime fiction, romance, literary fiction, thrillers, historical fiction... Each has its own conventions, or ways of writing and structuring.) There's no point beginning a detective novel, for example, with a description of a character's philosophical meanderings about what he wants for his breakfast. We want to get straight to the first murder. If you are writing something more dignified, you might want to think about how the setting and landscape can inform your themes.

BEST BEGINNINGS

It's a finely judged moment: you need to provide the reader with something recognizable, and yet also be original enough for their interest to be piqued.

The first lines of J. R. R. Tolkien's *The Hobbit*: "In a hole in the ground there lived a hobbit" and Philip Pullman's *The Golden Compass*: "Lyra and her daemon moved through the darkening hall..." show how to do this. Both contain enough that a reader can picture (hole, living, ground, moving, darkening, hall),

and yet surprise us with something new: what, we wonder, exactly is a hobbit, and what is a daemon and why does it belong to a girl with an odd name like Lyra? Both also subtly hint at the main plots: the hobbit will be yanked out of his hole to embark on an adventure, while *The Golden Compass* moves toward darkness and the north.

This technique is called foreshadowing, and you must learn it immediately if you want to be a good writer.

Go on, off you go and practice it!

Back? Good. Choosing where to start is a question of emphasis. Begin the story of Arthur with his birth out of wedlock, and you are foreshadowing the unhappy illegitimate birth of Arthur's son Mordred. Begin with Arthur's training in the castle of Sir Ector, and that would mean you are hinting at his martial prowess.

How, then, to start your own? You might have an idea of your overall plot.

Or you might feel as if you're groping in the dark. A beginning must set up the elements of the novel in a way that creates tension and excitement. It has to seize you by the lapel and ask, no, implore something of you.

You need a situation that invites change. Received writing opinion says you should start with a bang, and that's often taken to mean that you must begin with a literal explosion. I've lost track of the gazillions of manuscripts I've seen that take this advice to heart in exactly the wrong way. If you start with something that's too destructive, it will be confusing. Save the fireworks for the last act!

With the story of King Arthur, the idea of a boy suddenly finding out that he's the destined king of the land is gripping on an emotional level. You don't have to be a prince or even a boy to find it compelling, as we can all empathize with a sudden shift in circumstances.

Note that it's a small act that begins everything. Sir Kay leaves his sword in his lodgings: this forces Arthur to take the magical sword from the churchyard. In a way, it's Sir Kay's forgetfulness that makes Arthur king.

Consider your own plot. What's the small act, without which nothing would happen? Is it a decision to leave home without doing your homework that leads to you getting a detention that leads to you meeting your new best friend? Is it missing the bus and being forced to walk in the rain and finding a $10 bill on the sidewalk? Or is it the mysterious talking raven that perches on your windowsill in the morning and tells you that you need to find three magical rings before morning or the world will end?

EXPOSITION KLAXON!

Beginnings must avoid one particular thing: exposition. This is how characters arrived where they are now; how their world became like it is. When a piece of fiction sounded like it was too bogged down in explanatory bits, my creative writing students would shout EXPOSITION KLAXON!

Wanting to cram in shedloads of exposition is understandable: you've created a world, and so you demand that the reader knows all about it, right down to the most minute details. But too much exposition hampers beginnings.

The trick is to get to know your world well enough so that exposition becomes part of the natural behavior of your characters. Think about ways for such information to become inherent to the narrative. When you walk down your street, you don't think, "Ah, Nelson Avenue. Named after Admiral Lord Nelson, who won the Battle of Trafalgar..." Instead, you might think about sea battles, or Trafalgar Square, or some memory that you associate with the place. When your characters do the same, they should only notice things if they are directly relevant, or if they provide background information that has resonance or meaning in relation to the plot.

A good beginning should make us sympathize with the protagonist (the main character). This doesn' t mean that you have to lay on the woes with a trowel. The reader needs to be able to connect emotionally with what's going on. We also need a sense of location. Readers need something they can recognize. This can be as simple as

telling them that your protagonist is sitting in a chair. That chair might be on the deck of a pirate ship, or on a rocket heading off to Jupiter; but it's still a chair.

For the same reasons, you need a strong suggestion of time. Is it morning? Half past two? Think of the famous opening of George Orwell's *Nineteen Eighty-Four*, when the clocks start striking thirteen. It's brilliant because we can all work out what time it is from the chimes, but it also hints at something odd.

And then we need the movement which comes from the plot. Set those wheels in motion: you are the clockwork-maker, and you are turning the key... You can do this through foreshadowing, or through suggesting or anticipating an event. "Sarah was watching the cars passing her window, hoping her mother was in one" is a much better way to open a story than "Sarah woke up and yawned." TOP TIP: Never start a chapter with someone waking up. Just don't.

If, like King Arthur with his target practice, you hit the bullseye with all of the above in the first few paragraphs, then you'll be well on the way to creating a fantastic and gripping beginning. Draw your reader in. Entice them. Promise them things. Let a balloon rise up into the air: and see how it comes down. With a bang, we hope...

Over the next few pages, you'll find a summary of the story of King Arthur, and a series of suggestions to help you kick-start your writing and think, specifically, about beginnings.

So, sharpen your quills, dip them into the ink, and get writing.

the SWORD in the STONE

The legends of King Arthur are among the most compelling of all. They encompass chivalry, romance, wars, magic, quests, and tragedy; since the king's appearance in France and Britain, he has inspired many poems and novels. The gesture that starts everything is symbolic: the young boy Arthur pulls a sword out of a stone which, unknown to him, confers the kingship of the country, hurtling him into adulthood. The unknowing adds a vital layer of dramatic tension. The sword suggests Arthur's future as a warrior and the churchyard foreshadows his close relationship with Christianity and his own death.

THE STORY: IN A NUTSHELL

As a baby, Arthur was taken by the wizard Merlin to grow up with a foster father, Sir Ector. Unknown to him, his father was King Uther Pendragon and his mother the Queen of Cornwall.

The young Arthur was often overshadowed by his older brother, Kay. Far from the toil and troubles of London, it was Kay who got the best cuts of meat, the best horses, the best weapons.

When King Uther died, the lords were all called to the capital city for a tournament. On his way there, Kay realized that he'd left his sword at their lodgings, and sent Arthur back to retrieve it, only the house was shuttered up and locked.

Searching around, Arthur found a sword sticking out of a stone in a churchyard, drew it out with ease, and then brought it back to his brother. On asking where he had found it, Kay, Sir Ector, and Arthur returned to the churchyard, and read the inscription: "Whoever pulls this sword out of the stone will be King."

At first, nobody believed Arthur, but after he'd performed the feat several times, the barons accepted Arthur as their king.

Of course, it wasn't all hunky-dory after that. Arthur had to fight rebel kings; in some versions, he even defeated the Roman Emperor. He instituted his Round Table for his knights to show that they were all equal. They went on quests, slaying giants and following strange beasts. Arthur's wife Guinevere had an affair with the knight Lancelot; and, ultimately, all but Lancelot's son Galahad failed in the quest for the Holy Grail.

Arthur, at the last battle, was tragically slain by his own son Mordred. And all because he pulled a sword out of a stone.

TACKLE THE PROMPTS TO GET THINGS MOVING

1. EXPOSITION, EXPOSITION
Write down everything that's happened before the story starts. Think about how Arthur arrived in Ector's castle. Then write the beginning, with as little exposition as possible.

2. FORESHADOWING
Bearing in mind what happens to Arthur later in his life, can you foreshadow some events through objects or background?

3. THE SCISSORS TEST
Once you've started writing, cut out the first three paragraphs. Does the story now start in a more compelling way?

4. HUMBLE BEGINNINGS What if the wizard Merlin deposited Arthur in a poorer household, and he was brought up as a peasant boy? How would that change the beginning? Think about how the situation would shift into more dangerous territory: it would challenge order.

5. UPDATE THE STORY King Arthur is still asleep (see page 22), but one of his descendants is around. Where would he or she live? Explore a few different settings: it doesn't have to be London or even England. Could there be a descendant in the desert or the mountains, or in Australia? How could they prove who they are?

6. MAKE YOUR OWN LEGEND! King Arthur is part of the Matter of Britain (the body of stories and medieval romances that center around him). But can you invent a different legend? What if it wasn't a sword that had to be pulled out of a stone, but another object?

7. TRICKERY What if someone knew that Arthur was Uther's son, tricked him into taking the sword, and then got him out of the way?

8. THREE WAYS TO WRITE A BEGINNING Scribble the start of the story of King Arthur in three different ways, at three different points. Compare and contrast.

9. KAY'S STORY Imagine what it's like to be the older brother of the king. How would he feel when the baby Arthur is brought back? Think of this as another beginning.

10. FIFTEEN WAYS TO DESCRIBE A CASTLE Scribble down the first 15 words you associate with CASTLE. Do it without thinking. Then use those words for a couple of paragraphs in the beginning.

11. DIFFERENT TIMES Try writing the beginning of the story at different points in the day: morning, noon, and night. How does this affect the story in terms of its mood and propulsion?

KEY WORD
IN MEDIAS RES
Beginning right
in the middle of the
action.

Zzz

THE SLEEPING KING

Arthur's tombstone carries the latin words *Rex Quondam Rexque Futurus*: "The Once and Future King. He's not dead, merely asleep...."

LITTLE BEAR?
Many people think Arthur means "little bear." But it is more likely derived from the Latin name Artorius. The Roman commander Lucius Artorius Castus is a possible historical source for King Arthur.

KEY WORD
INCITING INCIDENT
Scriptwriters use this phrase: it means the event that puts everything in motion.

KEY WORD
STATUS QUO
How things are at the
beginning of the story.
How does your opening
disrupt the status quo?

CHAPTER TWO
CRAFTING

Writers! Yes, you! Know your characters! You must learn everything about them! Not just as if they were your most intimate friends. Probably even better, as you don't know exactly what your friends are thinking (unless you're telepathic, which, to be fair, you probably aren't. Are you?).

You probably have some idea of the characteristics of your fictional cast: age, height, ability to eat 15 chips in one go, and so on. Note these down. They will come in handy. But they are not everything.

You probably have a vague idea about where they live. This is very important too, and we'll talk about this more in Setting (see page 50). Character is in many ways born from setting, and the two interact in very important ways. But you probably haven't given much thought to the life stories of your fictional creations. Don't worry too much about this: characters evolve over time,

and the more effort you put into them, the more alive they will become.

Spend a few hours just hanging out with them. Catch them by surprise. Interview them, ask them what they want, what they need. Their motives will help you to understand both your plot and the setting.

CHARACTER

Your characters need goals: specific desires that will be fulfilled, or not. These can be epic: Frodo needs to destroy the ring! Or they can be on a much smaller scale: Samira needs to finish her art project by Tuesday or her mom will cancel her birthday party! Either way, it's our hopes and desires that help to make us, and in the same way, your characters, too.

DEVELOPING YOUR METHOD

All writers have different methods, and I'm by no means suggesting that you have to compose a birth-to-death biography of each character. That would be insane (although some people do it. Those people are insane). But it does help when you think about them deeply. And this can be a difficult thing to achieve. More often than not, I see characters who simply exist to move on the plot, or who are passive and let things happen to them.

Characters need to generate plot by what they do.

There are many ways to get into the right mindset. First of all, understand your characters in a normal situation.

Envisage your character going about daily life: bedroom, bathroom, house, routines. None of this needs to end up in your final work, but it helps to situate a character. How do they enter a room? Where do they feel most comfortable? What would irritate them, please them, anger them?

Let's say you're writing about Orpheus and Eurydice, the tragic legendary couple separated by death. What would their bedrooms be like? What do they do when they wake up in the morning? How can you foreshadow Eurydice's snakebite? Think about their daily routines: washing, dressing, eating breakfast.

Once you've got a few sketches, you'll find that you're thinking about your characters in a different way. Those shady outlines will be more filled in. This is an exciting time: your characters will start to live, and they will do things of their own accord when you let your mind rest. Jot down what they do: it will come in handy.

When you've got a sense of the characters' appearance and how they interact with the space around them, then decide what they want. What's their motivation? In the myth of Theseus and the Minotaur (see page 66), for example, Theseus is aiming to destroy the Minotaur and, with any luck, not get himself killed. There is no psychology, here, however: can you fill in some other motivations? How does Theseus feel about accepting the help of Ariadne? This will help shape your characters, and will also have a bearing on the plot.

The best characters are dynamic: they are full of energy, and that's usually because they want something or are trying to stop something from happening. The last thing you want is for your protagonist to be passive, to be carted about at the mercy of fate. They have to make decisions. Those decisions may be the wrong ones, of course. But there has to be a sense of vitality.

The protagonist is usually endowed with various positive virtues: courage, bravery, kindness, and so on. This can mean that they end up being something of a cipher (a character that feels flat); so it's important to give them other qualities. That might be a sense of conflict about their role, or it might be a particular talent or habit they possess, such as whistling or biting their nails.

Villains, or antagonists, are usually given negative traits, although a bizarre thing about them is that very often they are the most energetic characters and possibly even more creative than the protagonist. They want things too, but usually they're prepared to be selfish instead of altruistic in order to get them.

Many writers confess to enjoying writing about their villains more than their heroes. This has always been the case. For example, think how magnificently evil Cruella de Vil is in *The Hundred and One Dalmatians*, as opposed to the one-dimensional Dearlys.

Writing manuals often talk about "showing, not telling." When writing, it's very tempting to say, "Samantha was angry." It's a lot harder to show that anger through Samantha's actions. Try "Samantha slammed the door so hard that the paintings shook."

Of course, you need to be able to do both showing and telling. Being able to write confidently means being able to judge when you can summarize something: "The journey was long, and made Scarlett bored and irritable." Or when you need to delve into it more clearly because it is emotionally compelling or related to the plot. "Scarlett was idly playing with the handle of the train's window, when she saw, reflected behind her, that her neighbor was taking a dagger from under his coat...."

Observe. Research. Think about how characters develop over time. How does Hamlet go from being a rebellious prince to a revenger? Write down some thumbnail sketches of people you know in which you dissect their characters and characteristics. Hope that said friends never find your sketches. Maybe shred them, just in case. Scribble down how people react in a crisis. Does Ali stay calm while Ellie cowers in the corner?

CRAFTING AN ARC

Your character needs to have what those in the business call an "arc." If your protagonist just stayed the same all the way through the text, it would be no fun, would it? Many creative writing instructors and screenwriters think of it literally as an arc: the character goes from brave but shy to confident, via a series of tests. It's how your character changes inside: how outside events alter them.

I dislike being too formulaic, and I hope things are more complicated than that. Your character can suffer setbacks in every chapter, if you want, and those will lead them on to strengthening their resolve. This is where character becomes very closely related to plot and structure (as we'll soon see). Plot events are crucial in shaping your characters. That moment when your shy princess picks up her sword and realizes it's her destiny, for example; or when your battle-weary queen sees her last enemy approaching, and resolves that this will be her final moment of glory...

In the next few pages, we'll be looking in detail at the myth of Perseus and the Gorgon Medusa, and how we can develop the characters we find there. We'll then be discussing Odysseus and the Cyclops, and understanding how craftiness and heroism go alongside each other. Finally, we'll think about what it's like to be on the edge of things, when we meet Achilles' magical talking horses, who can give us a whole new perspective on the main events of the *Iliad*.

Also, remember that throughout the book, you can apply any of the things we discuss in each section to any of the other stories. Always remember: writing isn't schematic. You can break the rules, too.

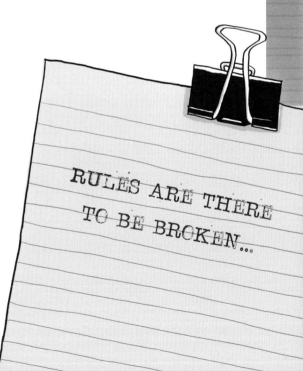

RULES ARE THERE TO BE BROKEN...

PERSEUS and ANDROMEDA

This ancient myth, and it is one of the most ancient of all the Greek myths, has everything: prophecies, monsters, love, and revenge. Note the careful way this myth is structured. The first half is a quest narrative in which a monster is overcome; it then ends on a note of hope and marriage. The second half ties up the loose ends from the beginning: the death of Polydectes and the fulfillment (in an unexpected way) of the prophecy. Every element of the story is essential. It's like a beautifully crafted piece of furniture.

THE STORY: IN A NUTSHELL

Perseus had a fairly troubled life: no sooner was he born than he and his mother Danaë were thrown into a box and cast out to sea. You may well ask why? Well, there had been a prophecy that Perseus would kill his grandfather. Mother and son landed in Seriphos, where they were taken in by King Polydectes. But when the king fell for Danaë, he decided to get rid of Perseus, and packed him off to slay the Gorgon Medusa.

This Perseus did, with the help of the gods Athena and Hermes, who gave him a magic sickle (to cut her head off); a cap of darkness (for invisibility); and winged shoes. Flying home, Perseus spied a maiden chained to a rock by the sea. This was Andromeda.

Andromeda's mother, Cassiopeia, was the Queen of the Ethiopians. She'd boasted that her daughter was more beautiful than the sea nymphs, and so they, being angered, asked Zeus to punish her, which he did, by flooding the land and calling up a giant sea monster. Andromeda's father, Cepheus, went to an oracle for help: the only way to get rid of the monster was to sacrifice Andromeda.

Enter Perseus, quite literally falling from the sky. He asked Andromeda first, and

then Cepheus, for her hand in marriage if he could slay the monster. Having already dispatched the Gorgon, you can imagine that Perseus was feeling a little confident. He managed to kill the monster, marry Andromeda, see off Phineus (her evil uncle), and have a son with Andromeda before taking her back with him to Greece. Here he turned Polydectes into stone and gave the Gorgon's head to Athena.

All was well, until Perseus attended some funeral games and, in throwing a discus, accidentally killed his own grandfather. See how none of the Greek heroes escape tragedy...

USE THE PROMPTS BELOW TO PRACTICE DEVELOPING CHARACTER THROUGH ACTION, MOTIVATION, AND SIGNIFICANT OBJECTS

1. CHARACTERISTICS: PERSEUS Handsome, bold, brave: the classic hero. You'd think Perseus would be a bit boring. But somehow, he's not: the fact that he's aided by Athena (intelligence) and Hermes (cunning) adds depth to him. Can we play with this a little? He's a tool of destiny—how might that change his reactions to the path that's set out for him?

2. DEVELOPING PERSPECTIVE Imagine Perseus as a little boy, growing up on Seriphos. He's watching his mother with the new king in the palace. How can you show Perseus' distrust of the king and his love for his mother? What can Perseus see? How does he interpret what he sees? Perhaps a hand on a wrist, a kiss declined or accepted, or a door slamming.

3. SHOWING THROUGH ACTION Rewrite the scene where Perseus chooses to save Andromeda so that it's her father who persuades him to do so. Show his character through his reactions, his actions, and his movements. What could the king offer Perseus?

DIVING DEEPER: TIME TO MYTH IT UP!
Andromeda is a princess of the Ethiopians. Reimagine the story in either one of the following ways:

4. ROLE REVERSAL It's Andromeda who has to go and slay Medusa, but with the help of two Ethiopian deities. On her return, she passes Greece where she sees Perseus tied to a rock: his father has boasted that he's more handsome than the Tritons, and Zeus is punishing them with a sea monster. What would Andromeda do in this situation?

5. MOTHERLY LOVE Give a voice to Cassiopeia, Andromeda's mother, a powerful queen. What cause may she have had to boast? What if Perseus didn't appear at all, and it was left to Cassiopeia to save Andromeda? How would Cassiopeia feel that it's her daughter who has to be sacrificed, and not herself? Might she offer up herself instead?

GRAB A PEN AND USE THE PROMPTS FROM THE PREVIOUS PAGE, OR THE EXTRA ONES BELOW, AND LET YOUR CREATIVITY FLOW!

6. BLENDED IDENTITY There is a famous sculpture of Perseus and the Head of Medusa by Cellini. Have a look at it. You'll see that Perseus very strongly resembles Medusa. What do you think this might suggest?

7. LISTS, LISTS, LISTS! One way of getting to know your characters is through lists. Make lists of the following for Perseus, Andromeda, Medusa, and Cassiopeia. First memory? Sounds heard when waking up? Favorite place? Favorite taste?

8. WORD ASSOCIATION Think of ten words for things that you associate with the sea monster. Then play around with these words. Is the monster a snaky beast? Or does it have tentacles? What's its weak spot, and how does Perseus kill it? Can it talk? Does it have unexpected magical powers?

KEY WORD
STEREOTYPE
A flat character
that fulfills
expectations.

IN THE STARS

All of the characters in the story of Perseus and Andromeda became constellations. You can see them in the night sky.

BLOODY BIRTH

The winged horse Pegasus sprang from the blood of the Gorgon's head. He was then captured by the hero Bellerophon, who rode on him to slay the monster Chimera. Bellerophon and Perseus are sometimes confused.

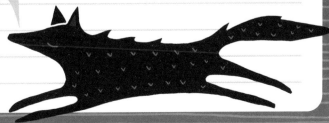

KEY WORD
FOIL
A character that highlights the qualities of your main character, through contrasting characteristics. Could Perseus have a sidekick?

ODYSSEUS and the CYCLOPS

Odysseus is the archetypal cunning hero. He even has his own poem, the *Odyssey*, which details his adventures as he returns from the destruction of the city of Troy. He combines a brilliant wit with strength and perseverance. When Odysseus and his men come up against the one-eyed giant Cyclops, he's pitted against a seemingly immovable brutality. We see Odysseus' character developing as he works out how to defeat the threat. He can't use brute force alone. So, what can he do?

THE STORY: IN A NUTSHELL

Troy was besieged for ten years by the Greek armies. Once the city was razed to the ground, the Greek leaders set off for home, laden with their spoils of war. But the journey wasn't as easy as they'd hoped, and Odysseus spent 20 years traveling home. Along the way, he met many fantastical creatures. The Cyclops is only one of them. The others include cannibalistic Laestrygonians; sirens who sing men to their deaths; lotus-eaters who exist in a state of permanent drugged happiness; and Scylla and Charybdis, the sea monster and the whirlpool between whom Odysseus must pass. There's plenty in this poem to play with.

Odysseus and his men land on an island, which seems to be inhabited by shepherds. They enter a cave and find it full of cheese. Hooray! Cheese all round! The only problem is that the owner of the cave returns and proves himself to be a one-eyed giant, the Cyclops Polyphemus. Annoyed at being invaded, Polyphemus shuts Odysseus and his crew in the cave and then proceeds to polish them off, two by two, every night, for his supper. When the Cyclops asks Odysseus who he is, he gives a false name: No-man.

Stymied, Odysseus considers his options. And then he has a brilliant idea. He and his men get Polyphemus drunk, and, when he's asleep and snoring, they poke his eye out with a stick. Enraged and blinded, the Cyclops threatens revenge. When he lets his sheep out of the cave, he checks each one as they leave. But Odysseus and his men lash themselves to the bellies of the sheep and get away, if not exactly scot-free, then freely enough, as the giant bellows after them that No-man has blinded him.

Odysseus sails away, but it is a long time before he reaches home, especially with the curse of Poseidon, the Cyclops' father. On reaching home, he finds his palace overrun by suitors pestering his wife Penelope for her hand in marriage. Disguised as a beggar, he slaughters them all, and he and Penelope are reunited.

USE THESE PROMPTS TO THINK MORE ABOUT CHARACTER

INTO THE CAVE
It's all about Odysseus, but what about the Cyclops? He's minding his own business, after all.

1. INCONGRUITY Pick three photographs from a magazine, and put the Cyclops in each one. Write how he got there.

2. GIRLS RULE There are many female characters in the *Odyssey*, but none in the story of the Cyclops. What would it be like if the Cyclops were Polyphema? Or if a member of Odysseus' crew were a girl disguised as a boy?

3. EIGHT WAYS TO WRITE ABOUT THE SEA Do a word association: speed-write the first eight words you think of when you think about the sea, and then personify it (give it human qualities).

4. POLYPHEMUS IS POLYPHEMUS BECAUSE... Write down a list of ten objects or moments in the Cyclops' life that made him who he is. Sample: "I am a sheepherder..."

5. WRITE YOUR OWN! Think of the Cyclops as a symbol of something more: What could the Cyclops represent? And how could your protagonist overcome it?

KEY WORD
ANTAGONIST
Someone who comes up
against the protagonist,
causing conflict. *Agon* in
Ancient Greek means
"a conflict."

KEY WORD
CRISIS
Your character should
have a moment of crisis.
Usually it's brought on by
external events.

WHO'S WHO?
The Roman name for
Odysseus is Ulysses.

TRAGIC TWIST
Odysseus is
accidentally killed
by his own son,
Telegonus.

ACHILLES' MAGICAL HORSES

One of my favorite moments in Homer's epic poem, the *Iliad*, is when Achilles' horses, Xanthus and Balius (who are, naturally, magical) weep because they see his future death. I've always been fond of them because they are so close to the main hero. They take him out to fight, sleep near his tent, and have special knowledge about him. One of the most poignant things about their story is that once they've been given the gift of speech, it is taken away from them as soon as they've finished their prophecy. They watch from the sidelines, powerless. But perhaps it's time to give them some power of their own... Think about how characters on the edges of the main story can help to throw the major characters into relief. Sometimes you can get to know your own characters better simply by writing them from someone else's point of view.

THE STORY: IN A NUTSHELL

With Greek myth, you find yourself always coming back to the marriage of the hero Peleus and the sea nymph Thetis: it seems to start everything. All the gods and heroes came to the wedding, and Poseidon, the god of the sea, gave the enchanted horses to Peleus in celebration. Even before Achilles was born, the horses were there. Achilles may even have learned to ride on one, or both of them. He would have grown to know them and love them, hacking about the countryside or hunting in the woods.

Thetis didn't want Achilles to fight in the Trojan War, and so sent him off (disguised as a girl) to the island of Scyros; it is not written whether his horses went with him. Eventually, Achilles was discovered by Odysseus, and he and his horses were packed off to join the fray, along with Patroclus, Achilles' companion and best friend.

The Trojan War dragged on for ten years, as the Greek forces besieged the city. Achilles was their best fighter, leading them on to victory after victory, raiding the surrounding towns, and generally being a hero.

And then when Achilles withdrew from battle over a slight to his honor, and Patroclus fought in his place, the latter died in battle, and the horses wept at his death. On their return, Achilles told them off: how could they have let his best friend die? But then the goddess Hera granted them the gift of speech and prophecy, and they told of Achilles' death, before being struck mute once more.

GIVE THE STORY A TWIST BY FOCUSING ON CERTAIN CHARACTERS

1. EQUINE WORLD Imagine you're one of the horses, and tell the story of the day you find out that Achilles is going to die. Think about being a horse: the sights, the smells, the sounds.

2. CONFLICTS OF CHARACTER Imagine that the horses argue over something. Do they think Achilles loves one more than the other?

3. PEACE, NOT WAR The *Iliad* is about war, but what if the horses refused to pull the chariots? Describe the scene. Are they afraid? Do they confront their fears?

4. SIX WAYS TO BLITZ A BATTLE Do a speed word association around SPEAR, and construct a paragraph around the words. Use this to start a story in which the horses appear.

5. WRITE YOUR OWN! Invent magical companions for any one of the characters in the Trojan War. What if Helen had a talking peacock? Or Hector a magical leopard?

KEY WORD
ARISTEIA
In Homer's *Iliad*, an *aristeia* is the section when a hero goes out into battle for glory.

KEY WORD
ARCHETYPE
An overarching type of character, such as a villain, a damsel in distress, or a hero.

LONELY MONSTER
There are no composite animals in the *Iliad*, apart from the Chimera (goat head, lion head, snake head).

CHAPTER THREE

SETTING

Location, location, location! You are a person passing through space: how do you affect it, and how does it affect you? Do you sashay? Do you stomp? Do you wriggle? Do you romp?

Readers often say that setting is as much of a character as, well, the characters. When I think about the Minotaur, I don't just think of him as a monstrous, shapeless embodiment of evil, pacing the stone floor of his labyrinth. He can be that, but you can do more with him.

I think about where he sleeps: does he have a blanket? As he is the son of the queen, was it once a rich piece of linen,

now ragged and torn with age? Does he sleep on the rough stone, or has he found somewhere more comfortable?

The Minotaur knows the labyrinth intimately: he could tell you the different shades in the rock as you near the entrance, or the darker places near the center. He can sense the currents of air when the huge doors open, bringing a fresh tribute to him. He knows where he should wait, just where the darkness of the fourth turn becomes a blank wall, where the unwary falter... He crumples the blanket in his hand, and remembers his first kill...

Sorry, got carried away there. Back to it.

I always use the term "anchorage" when I talk about setting. Readers need something to hold them down, and your characters must be firmly placed in their settings. They need drapes, kitchens, spoons, and windows (even on spaceships or at the bottom of the sea. In fact, especially on spaceships or at the bottom of the sea). They need objects that are meaningful to them, and only to them. A chipped blue bowl, given by a now-dead grandmother. A tin box containing a child's first hair clippings. A sword kept vigorously clean.

Think about your protagonist: she lives in a cottage at the edge of the forest; she has a vase of flowers she's picked herself on her mantelpiece. Your antagonist, on the other hand, lurks in a mansion in the middle of the forest; she never picks flowers but has them sent to her at great expense.

ATMOSPHERICS

Atmosphere is crucial in fostering an emotional connection with your reader: the gloomy approach to the deserted mansion; the glittering mirrors in the fairy palace; the cozy warmth of a fire in the bedroom under the eaves. As with character, detail is best. If you lay on the adjectives too broadly and thickly, you will have the opposite effect to what you intend. Sometimes, a tiny detail, such as a flag fluttering at half-mast, or a fall leaf on a lawn, can do a lot.

Myths and folktales provide as many beautiful, involving settings as there are places in the world (and beyond). They are rooted in landscapes. Imagine the Ancient Greek heroes sailing around the Mediterranean and eventually reaching the edges of their known worlds. Remember the hero Peleus on the *Argo*, cleaving through the watery main, and his first sight of the sea nymph Thetis.

Think of the djinns in the deserts of Arabia, or perhaps the ice giants in the far north in Norse myth. King Arthur's stories firmly planted him in the landscape of Britain: so much so that today we still point at his Round Table in Winchester. Despite this connection to the landscape, the solid bones of the stories mean they can be transferred anywhere—*Aladdin*, for example, which most of us think of as being very much Arabian, is actually set in China.

When you're thinking about your setting, remember that each place has resonances. A deep dark wood is going to suggest mystery and enchantment. Mountains beg to be climbed. A cityscape is full of unexpected wonders as well as serious troubles. Places that are on the edges are fascinating: a shoreline is in between the sea and the land. Boundaries are made to be dissolved and crossed.

Draw maps, even if you're as bad at drawing as I am. You can always leave a big X for Unknown... that will make you consider it even more. If you draw a map of your protagonist's house, include words and memories for each particular space.

If you're stuck for a storyline, make notes about your setting. Write down what your protagonist can see from a window. Picture your protagonist being uprooted from one place to another, and the story will flow. There's always a reason for moving, and it means that storylines open up. Journeys—making your way through landscape—become psychological journeys too, as adventures to overcome, to strengthen (or weaken) character. Sometimes, making something strange can make your work come alive.

HIT THE SENSES

You need to hit up all the senses. This is where research comes in. This can take many forms. It can mean sitting in a local café, picking up the atmosphere. What smells are coming from the kitchen? What's on the tables? Are there strollers by the door, or is there an old man in an overcoat reading the paper? Think about food: that helps to anchor us in one place.

Really getting to know a place can help your writing immeasurably: see Alan Garner's love of the Cheshire landscape, which comes through so powerfully in his work. Ride the bus routes around your town or city. Look at how the streets change. Write down names, streets, and images. Go for a walk up and down your street, noting things you never thought you would notice: the texture of the asphalt, the colors of the front doors,

the windows left half open, the dinners being cooked….

At the other extreme, you can travel all across the world: the writer Michelle Paver is known for her trips to the far north, which help bring her novels alive.

If you can't travel, don't worry! We do, after all, have our imaginations. Leaf through books, or browse the Internet. Compile dossiers and files. Become a spy, a cartographer, a sociologist. Be nosy. Notice everything. It will all be useful. If you're writing about somewhere else, look at maps, travel books, local histories: try to understand the landscape and its role in shaping the lives of its inhabitants.

Fantasy landscapes must have coherence, and this goes right down to the naming of places. Don't just collect together a random group of words. Think about etymologies: the way that words and names become themselves. Look at how place names grew up around you. What does Edinburgh mean? or Sydney, or Vienna? All location names have meanings. Consider how you can do this in your fantasy world. White Fort could become Whitfort.

J. R. R. Tolkien hardly moved from Oxford, and yet he was a past master at landscape. Each section of Middle Earth has symbolic power: the Shire, where the hobbits live, is rural England. The hobbits don't like adventure, and their houses and habits reflect that. Rohan, with its plains, horses, and kingly halls, is Anglo-Saxon; Gondor represents urban sophistication and decadence.

Setting can provide a foil for your character. Perhaps your protagonist grows up in a small suburb and finds it oppressive, longing for the bright lights and big cities. Perhaps your protagonist is in the big city and longs for the countryside. Writers have used these techniques for as long as there have been writers: landscape, for example, is all-important in the *Odyssey,* where Odysseus longs for the safe civilization of his homeland, instead having to endure the privations of the landscape.

One of the best exercises you can do to learn how to use setting in your writing is to rewrite scenes through different emotional lenses. Take your protagonist and imagine him or her waking up. Is there something exciting happening that day? Something terrifying? How does your character react to ordinary objects? Let's say you wake up on the morning of an exam: your alarm clock or phone will be nagging at you; your clothes might feel a little more uncomfortable than usual, the bus to school more sinister...

Over the next few pages, we'll look at one of the stories about Baba Yaga, the terrifying witch from Russian folktale, and think about how landscape informs that particular story. We'll also visit the trickster Soongoo'ra in his African home. And we'll grapple with the mighty Minotaur in his labyrinthine lair. All the time we'll be thinking carefully about how landscape can live and set off character, while providing plot too.

Go forth, observe, and explore!

Baba Yaga's hut is supported by chicken's legs.

BABA YAGA and VASILISA

Russia's old forests and steppes provide a gloomy location for folklore. Baba Yaga, a terrifying witch who lives in a house made of chicken's legs surrounded by a fence of human bones, haunts thousands of tales. Sometimes she's cannibalistic; other times she's helpful. Baba Yaga is an ambiguous character who represents wildness and ancient magic. *Baba* means "old woman" and *Yaga* may mean anything from "horrible" to "rider" to "witch." The setting in her stories provides both psychological resonance and a suitable space for adventures.

THE STORY: IN A NUTSHELL

Vasilisa's dying mother gave her a doll. If Vasilisa was ever in need of help, she should give it food and drink, and the doll would help her. Her father remarried, as fathers always do in fairy tales, and the new stepmother and her two daughters inevitably made Vasilisa's life a misery. They moved to a hut in the forest.

One day, the stepmother put out all the lights in the house, except for one candle, and told Vasilisa to go the forest and fetch fire from Baba Yaga's hut. Terrifying and capricious, Baba Yaga lived in a house with chicken's legs at each corner, which could get up and run about; she traveled in a large pestle and mortar. Vasilisa went to the hut, and was given the choice of working for Baba Yaga or being put to death. She chose to clean, cook, and wash. One day, Baba Yaga gave Vasilisa an impossible task: she must

separate poppy seeds from soil. Exhausted, Vasilisa gave the doll some food and drink and slept while the doll completed the tasks. On her return, Baba Yaga asked Vasilisa how on earth she had managed it. She answered: "With my mother's blessing," which was entirely the right thing to say, as it turned out, because Baba Yaga, in a rage, sent her back home. Vasilisa left, bearing a skull full of coals—she needed a flame, after all.

When she returned to the cottage, she found that in her absence, they hadn't been able to strike a flame. The skull-fire burned up the stepmother and her daughters. Hooray! Vasilisa spent the rest of her life with her father, or went on to marry the Tsar of Russia. Either way, she was happy. And, we expect, the doll was too.

USE THE PROMPTS BELOW TO CREATE DIFFERENT SETTINGS AND LOCATIONS

1. INTO THE FOREST Write about the moment when Vasilisa first enters the woods and sees Baba Yaga's hut. How do you show her surprise and fear, and increase that using the landscape? What details can you add to the hut to make it even more terrifying?

2. INSIDE THE HUT Think about how you can describe the interior of Baba Yaga's hut. What is bubbling away in the cauldron?

3. HUT LOCATION Pick one of the following locations for Baba Yaga's hut to land in: Ancient China, the top of the Eiffel Tower, or a colony in space in the year 4000. Or come up with your own.

4. I, HUT! Baba Yaga's hut must have a lot of stories to tell. How would it feel about Vasilisa coming in? Write a short piece.

5. SPARK OFF A TALE Use the following list of words to kick-start a story: pestle, skull, fox, herbs, knife, binoculars...

6. FOREST OF FEAR Think of the largest, most terrifying forest you can. Describe it in as much detail as possible. Then use that to spark off another Baba Yaga story.

7. CHOOSE A MOTIF Pick one of these two objects from Baba Yaga's hut: the skull or the doll. Then use the object as a motif (see page 59) in your story in an unexpected way.

8. BABA YAGA'S FLIGHT Baba Yaga rides in a pestle and mortar. Write down the sights, sounds, and smells she experiences as she flies through the woods.

KEY WORD
PSYCHOGEOGRAPHY
How setting precisely
affects character
and emotions.

MOTIF
You can use landscape
and setting for a motif,
which is a recurring idea
or image in a story.

the HARE and the LION

This story is about the trickster Soongoo'ra the hare. Note how landscape is acutely important here: the calabash tree in the forest, which Soongoo'ra climbs, showing his mastery of the surroundings; the use of the straw to hide the hare, again showing a versatile cunning in using what's available; the mountainous new home for Soongoo'ra, which shows the lengths he'll go to to hide; and the lion's eventual, exhausted return home, beaten by the hare.

THE STORY: IN A NUTSHELL

Soongoo'ra, a lithe and intelligent hare, was searching for his breakfast one morning when he found a beehive in the branches of a calabash tree that belonged to Simba the lion.

Soongoo'ra spotted Boo'koo, the rat, and told him that his father had bequeathed him a hive of honey, and could Boo'koo help? "Well, of course," answered the rat.

Only, after they've smoked out the bees and begun their feast, Simba the lion appeared. He was not pleased and asked them both to come down.

Soongoo'ra asked the rat to wrap him up in straw and throw him out of the tree, which the rat did; Soongoo'ra managed to get away, while Simba dispatched the rat.

A bit later, Soongoo'ra tried the same trick on Kobay the tortoise. Kobay was a bit brighter, however, than the rat and suspected the hare; so when Soongoo'ra asked him to do the hay trick, Kobay called down to Simba and warned him that the hare was coming down. "Don't eat me," said the hare. "Spin me around by the tail, and knock me out."

The lion did but the dastardly hare managed to sneak away, and the disappointed lion couldn't even eat the tortoise.

Soongoo'ra whizzed off to a new house on top of a mountain. Simba found the house while Soongoo'ra was away, and the hare, returning and seeing his tracks, called out: "Hello house, how are you!" When there was no answer, he said, "How strange, the house always answers me!" At which point Simba answered in the voice of the house. Soongoo'ra burst out laughing and ran away.

Simba couldn't be bothered to chase him; completely exhausted, he gave up, returning to his calabash tree while Soongoo'ra got off completely scot-free.

EXPLORE HOW SETTING CAN INFORM CHARACTER AND PLOT

1. USE THOSE SENSES Describe the first time Soongoo'ra finds the beehive. Think especially about honey and write down what you associate with it.

2. TWIST IT UP! What creature could outwit a hare? Could Soongoo'ra get his comeuppance? What landscape features might help toward that?

3. SHIFT THE STORY What would happen if the creatures were transposed to a modern, urban setting? Imagine Soongoo'ra slinking around the streets of Paris, London, New York...

4. SUBSIDIARY CHARACTERS Choose one of the minor characters, then write a story in 100 words based on the disruption to their life.

5. SIMBA AT HOME Write down Simba's life in food. What's his earliest memory of eating? What makes him gag? What does he eat to celebrate?

BEDTIME STORIES
African folktales are sometimes called "tales by moonlight."

TRICKY TALES
The trickster is a common feature of African folktales: Anansi the spider, Ogo-Yuruga the pale fox, and the Mantis of the San.

KEY WORD
SCENE SHIFT
How you help the reader
to understand that the
character is moving.

THESEUS and the MINOTAUR

The labyrinth is one of the greatest settings in myth: a seemingly endless maze with a monster lurking at the heart of it. Psychologically intense, as well as gripping in and of itself, the confines of the corridors, the darkness, the flickering torchlight, all combine to create tension and terror. Like all Greek myths, there is a heavy element of tragedy in the story of Theseus: the hero's actions are complicated by his treatment of Ariadne and by his pride in conquering the monster. Enjoy delving deep into the darkness.

THE STORY: IN A NUTSHELL

The Minotaur, the half-man/half-bull, was born in the Palace of Knossos on the island of Crete after Queen Pasiphae conceived an unnatural passion for a bull. Out of shame, King Minos and Pasiphae ordered the craftsman Daedalus to construct the famous labyrinth in order to conceal the monster: a maze that would confuse anyone who entered it.

Meanwhile, as a tribute, the Cretans demanded the sacrifice of youths from Athens to the Minotaur every year. This practice went on for quite some time, with the Athenians losing their brightest and best.

One year, Theseus, the Prince of Athens, asked his father Aegeus if he could go: he wanted to stop the sacrificial practice. "Yes," said Aegeus. "If you succeed, make sure to change your black sails to white before you arrive back home." Theseus set off to Crete, where Ariadne, the daughter of King Minos, fell in love with him.

Ariadne gave Theseus a ball of yarn to follow (called a "clew"—the origin of our word clue). Theseus entered the maze, found the Minotaur, and slew him.

It didn't end there. Theseus and Ariadne fled the island, and Theseus—either on purpose or because he was under the influence of a god or a spell—abandoned Ariadne on the island of Naxos where she was picked up by the god Dionysus.

Theseus sailed back to Athens, but he forgot to change his sails from black to white. When his father Aegeus saw the ship approaching, he threw himself to his death.

Theseus arrived home to find that he had become king of Athens and an orphan.

EXAMINE HOW SETTING AFFECTS ATMOSPHERE

1. BUILD YOUR OWN LABYRINTH First draw a plan of the labyrinth, and then write a simple description of it. Think about what kind of stone is used, how dark it is, how cold it is. Then rewrite the paragraph from the point of view of the labyrinth's maker, Daedalus.

2. WHAT THE MINOTAUR KNOWS Choose five places in the labyrinth, and associate them with five different points in the Minotaur's life: the first time he arrives; finding a place to sleep; first tribute; tenth tribute; and, finally, death.

3. MOVE THE LABYRINTH! Place the labyrinth on the side of a volcano, under the sea, in the frozen wastelands of the north...

4. LOSE A SENSE Describe the inside of the labyrinth using only four of the five senses, without either sight or sound.

5. SIX WAYS TO BUILD A LABYRINTH... What if it wasn't made of stone, but of ice, or wood, or fire, or living trees, or magic... Write down six things, choose three, and write about them.

LABYRINTHINE MYSTERY
Some people think the labyrinth is the Palace at Knossos, on the island of Crete.

LEAPING BULLS
The practice of bull-leaping is thought to be the origin of the Minotaur story.

CHAPTER FOUR

VOICE, STYLE,

Your narrative voice is what makes your writing unique. It's like a fingerprint, or how your hair falls over your eyes, or the mole on your right cheek, or the way that you say "Er, yeah."

Some writers have such distinctive narrative voices that you can tell it is their writing from a single paragraph. Look at the rich, strange vocabulary of Frances Hardinge and the pared-back brilliance of Ernest Hemingway.

The best thing about voice is that the opportunities are endless. You can craft beautifully long, gorgeously sculpted sentences that drift and flow with the ebb and rise of your thoughts.

Or you can be brief. Concise.

Brutal.

You can try to write sentences that breathlessly don't have any punctuation at all.

Or, perhaps, if you are feeling more expansive, you can experiment with a bit more, shall we say, circumlocution, if you know what I mean. Or you can write with a lot of conjunctions and that will make your writing both relentless and compelling and... You get the picture.

You can delve into the richness of a dictionary, turning up gems like mouldiwarp, syzygy, and ichor.

Or you can be clean, colloquial.

You can riffle through the delights of a thesaurus (which is actually the Greek word for "treasure"), or you can seek, comb, ransack or rummage, through it.

You can use the latest slang, the words and phrases that you hear out on the streets and around you. It's up to you. Your style is you.

CLARITY IS KEY

Try to avoid too many abstract nouns, and use concrete nouns when you can. Clarity and precision should be the words you live by. Engrave them somewhere suitable.

Fiction needs to be grasped by the mind, to paint a picture that is easily envisaged. That's the great balance: your

and PERSPECTIVE

style must be your own, but it must also not get in the way of the reader.

What voice will you use, and why? The voice needs to suit the genre you're writing in (unless, of course, you're playing a very clever game; we'll leave that aside).

Ask yourself these questions: Who's telling this narrative, and why?

The standard storytelling perspective, which has been tried and tested over the centuries, is the third person omniscient narrator. In this, the narrator knows everything: you are a god, peering into people's hearts and minds. The power, the power! You can do anything!

Ahem. Sorry. More common today for fiction is the third person limited, where what is described is limited to the perspective of the protagonist, or the first person. Each one has its own difficulties and advantages.

If you opt for the third person, watch out for perspective shifts, which are common in first drafts. The jury is out on

them: I don't particularly mind them, and if you look at many writers from the past century, they don't seem to mind them either. People who don't like this call it head-hopping. Editors today prefer to avoid too many perspective shifts in third person limited.

Let's look at a couple of examples, and then you can decide and experiment for yourself:

THIRD PERSON OMNISCIENT:

"Arthur dawdled into the bedchamber, feeling very sorry for himself. Guinevere, seeing this, dropped her work and rushed to his side, hoping to be able to cheer him up. Outside, the rain battered the trees, sending the workmen home to their wives and welcome supper...."

The narrator here can see into both Arthur and Guinevere's minds, as well as those of the workmen outside.

THIRD PERSON LIMITED:

"Arthur dawdled into the bedchamber, feeling very sorry for himself. Guinevere dropped her work and rushed to his side. The rain battered the windows, and Arthur stared out, watching the workmen as they ran for cover..."

This paragraph is limited to what Arthur can see and know; the reader is left to infer what Guinevere is thinking from the way that she rushes to him, as well as where the workmen are going. You can see the advantages of doing it this way. While the omniscient narrator provides a wider viewpoint, the third person limited feels more intimate and sometimes more alive.

FIRST PERSON:

"I dawdled into the bedchamber, feeling very sorry for myself. I saw Guinevere was working there, doing that sewing she always does; she flung it aside and ran straight to me. I didn't want to be comforted, so I ignored her, going to the windows and looking out into the rain..."

Immediately you can see the problems here. Does this sound like King Arthur? What kind of voice would he have? Do you use a courtly register:

"I entered the bedchamber, whereupon my sorrow didst reveal itself...."

Or do you try to make it sound more natural? The problems multiply. You've got to try things out until they feel right.

When it does work out, it will feel completely natural, and you will find that things flow and flow. But if they don't, do not fear. All writers agonize over sentences and getting the voice just right. We tear our hair out. We bite our nails. We cross things out and try again and again and again until it's right.

CHOOSING YOUR VOICE

With a first person narrative, consider what it is that you're writing. Are you giving the reader unfettered access to the mind of your creation? Or is this an artifact, something written by your character: a diary, or a notebook, or some other kind of record? If the latter, then that can be fun to play with too, as it can mean your narrator is reliable or unreliable. An unreliable narrator will be playing games with the truth, revealing things to you in a particular order; this can lead to a great twist at the end when knowledge of the whole is revealed.

When thinking about your characters and their voices, you can keep notes about the words you associate with them. Each character will have their own voice, which will come through in dialogue too (we'll discuss this in the next chapter). This collection of words and phrases can help you to differentiate them. Aunt Theodora says, "Come along now!", Cousin Jasper always starts his sentences with "Maybe..." and Ermintrude, the nextdoor neighbor, tuts whenever she opens her mouth.

The most important thing to do is to practice. The poet Ted Hughes used to write out passages of writers he admired (William Shakespeare, Jonathan Swift.) This is actually a good place to start: you can find a paragraph from your favorite book that really moves you, and copy it out. See where the nouns and verbs sit, where the adjectives go, if adverbs are used: look at the actual nuts and bolts of the words on the page, how they are arranged for effect. Then try to write a scene in the style of the author. This is a fun exercise in itself.

Once you become practiced, you will find that you develop your own voice. You will notice your own peculiar tics, certain words that pop up too many times, certain phrases you overuse. It's a painful process, and one that gets harder and harder. But do not despair! You will only get better as you practice.

There are many things you can do to practice on a sentence level. Let's try something now. Look at the room around you, or the park, or the airplane, or wherever you're reading this. (If you're on a submarine, or on top of the Eiffel Tower, or in the rain forest, then I envy you.) Write a short paragraph describing it from an omniscient point of view.

Now try to describe it from a third person limited point of view, in the eyes of someone who knows the room well.

And now do the same, as if someone else has just seen it for the first time.

Now remove the senses: describe it only using sound, or sight, or smell.

And now in words of only two syllables or less.

You should see that you now have several different versions of what is essentially the same room.

Always think about this when you write. Over the next few pages, we will visit Japan, where you'll find the story of Izanagi and Izanami; we will descend to the bottom of the ocean and the drowned country of Atlantis; and to a fairy-tale Ancient Rome.

Wherever you go, consider carefully the voice and the style that you're using. Watch where you put your words and what order they go in.

You'll soon find that you're developing your own voice.

And that will take you to places you've never dreamed of.

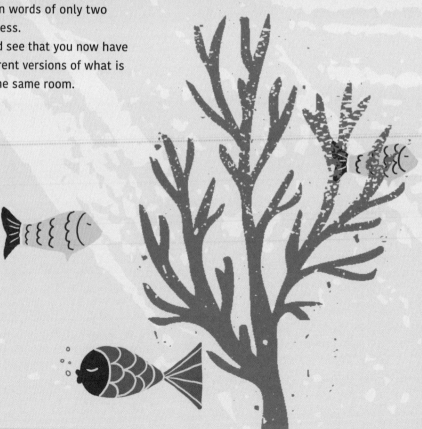

The Island of Atlantis sank beneath the waves after its people enraged the gods.

IZANAGI and IZANAMI

This gorgeous origin myth from Japan has many parallels with Greek myth. The hero descending to the Underworld: the taboo against eating there. The possibilities it opens up for developing different kinds of voices are immense, as almost the entire universe is the scene. You can try to write with a historical voice, with courtly overtones, or make it more colloquial and modern. You can develop the different voices of the gods and their progeny; you can explore the depths of the emotions that arise.

THE STORY: IN A NUTSHELL

Twins Izanagi and Izanami are the last of seven generations of gods. They create the Earth by stirring the waters with a glittering, jeweled spear. When they marry, their first child, Hiruko, is born imperfect thanks to a breach of protocol in the marriage ceremony. When they perform the ceremony again in the correct order, with the husband speaking first, Izanami gives birth to the Japanese archipelago. But when Izanami goes into labor with the fire god Kagutscuchi, she dies, throwing Izanagi into a terrible rage. He kills Kagutscuchi, and more gods arise from his remains and from the tears of Izanami.

Grief-stricken, Izanagi journeys to the Underworld where he promises that he will not look at Izanami. Izanami has already eaten food, which means she can't return with him. He looks at her and finds she has become a corpse. He flees.

Izanami sends the hags of Yomi (the Underworld) after him; Izanagi distracts them by throwing down a vine and a comb that holds his hair, which become bamboo and grapes. Izanagi then manages to escape, and he seals Izanami in the Underworld. She vows to kill 1,000 people a day; he vows to beget 1,500 people a day. And so begins the world...

CHANGE THE VOICE

1. ANCIENT EULOGY Protocol is very important in Japanese myth. Imagine the scene where Izanagi finds his wife dead. Try writing his speech of lamentation in a courtly manner.

2. GO MODERN Now try writing the same speech in a direct, modern way.

3. SWITCH NARRATIVE VOICE Write the opening paragraph in third person omniscient, third person limited, and first person. Choose which one fits best.

4. ANGRY RANT Write Izanami's speech of rage after being sealed into the Underworld.

5. SWAP THE STORY! Reverse the roles of Izanagi and Izanami. Instead of the death of Izanami, have Izanagi die at the hands of the fire god. Now write using Izanami's voice.

KEY WORD
DIEGESIS
The world in which
these narrated events
and other elements
occur.

KEY WORD
MIMESIS
The representation of
reality in fiction.

DIVINE BIRTH

The Imperial Japanese family claims descent from the sun goddess Amaterasu.

GODLY HORDES
There are at least eight
million gods and goddesses
in the Japanese pantheon.

PARTHENIA and ARGALUS

Sir Philip Sidney's *Arcadia* is an enchanting, complicated Elizabethan narrative: one of the first novels, set in a never-never version of Ancient Greece. Its main plot sees two princes, Musidorus and Pyrocles, falling in love with two princesses, Pamela and Philoclea; only Musidorus and Pyrocles are disguised, one as a shepherd and the other as an Amazonian. Both the king and the queen fall in love with Pyrocles; the former thinking he's a girl, the latter knowing that he isn't. The novel is jam-packed with subplots, including that of Parthenia and Argalus.

THE STORY: IN A NUTSHELL

Argalus, a drop-dead gorgeous knight, was also brainy and valiant. He fell in love with the equally beautiful and brainy Parthenia. Two problems arose: one, she was already in love with Argalus' best friend Clitophon; two, more seriously, she'd been promised by her mother to the proud, rich, and selfish Demagoras.

Parthenia chose Argalus as he was the kindest and most handsome knight. Her mother decided to try to remove him from the equation, and made him perform all sorts of labors before she died out of pure spite.

Argalus and Parthenia were then all set to marry, and Argalus returned home to collect his relations for the wedding. In his absence, Demagoras attacked Parthenia, rubbing a poison over her face, which made her look like a leper.

Argalus returned to find Parthenia disfigured. His love for her, however, was so strong that he insisted on marrying her, deferring his revenge on Demagoras.

Parthenia, however, refused. Thinking herself no longer worthy of him, she gave him his liberty. Argalus refused it, and Parthenia, weeping, stole away.

Devastated, Argalus searched for Parthenia for a long time, and then sought his revenge on Demagoras, who captured him and kept him alive.

Eventually, Argalus was rescued and returned to Clitophon's house. A message arrived: a strange young girl wanted to stay the night, and to speak publicly with Argalus. She was a dead ringer for Parthenia. Argalus was delighted. The stranger said that she merely looked very like Parthenia; the dying Parthenia had told her that Argalus' affection should be switched to her. The distraught Argalus refused: his heart belonged to Parthenia, though she was dead.

The girl then revealed herself as the real Parthenia. A physician cured her and she then devised the trial to test Argalus' love. They married, but they didn't live happily ever after, with both ending up as casualties of the war in Arcadia.

USE THESE PROMPTS TO SHIFT THE STORY'S PERSPECTIVE

1. GREEN-EYED MONSTER Parthenia sees Clitophon first and is then shoved out of the way in favor of Argalus. Write the moment when Argalus and Parthenia first meet, in the voice of Clitophon.

2. RUNNING AWAY Write Parthenia's speech to Argalus when she decides to flee, trying to differentiate her voice from Clitophon's. Make it psychologically convincing. What reasons might she have? Why does she refuse him?

3. CHANGE NARRATIVE APPROACH Write the opening of the story in a third person narration, in as courtly a manner as possible. Then write another, in a colloquial and modern narration. Which works better?

4. KEEP IT CONCISE Write the middle of the story using short, punchy sentences and avoiding abstract nouns such as confusion, hope, surprise, love, or anger (see page 87).

5. HAPPY ENDING While both Parthenia and Argalus die as a result of war in Arcadia, imagine a future for them in which they don't. Write a happy ending for them.

KEY WORD
ASYNDETON
Sentences that don't have any conjunctions (and, but, or, yet), piling on the clauses, creating a sense of breathlessness.

A HERO'S DEATH
Sir Philip Sidney died in battle,
at the age of 31. He refused a
cup of water, saying it should
go to one of his soldiers
who needed it more.

ATLANTIS

It is always compelling to imagine civilizations existing in unusual circumstances. The story of the fictional island of Atlantis, which comes from the dialogues of the Athenian philosopher Plato, tells of a great island city that sank under the waves. It has since become shorthand for underwater cities; many forget the original reason why it sank. Plato tells us that Critias heard it from his grandfather, who was told the story by the politician Solon, who heard it from an Egyptian priest.

THE STORY: IN A NUTSHELL

The great island of Atlantis was located somewhere beyond the Pillars of Hercules. Poseidon gave the island to his son, Atlas, and the civilization grew in prosperity and culture. It became advanced and luxurious. The Atlanteans grew more and more powerful, until they wished to conquer new worlds. So, off their ships and armies went, storming through the lands of Europe and Africa, and eventually begetting an empire that spanned Egypt and Italy. (The Athenians, of course, were meant to have driven them away; don't forget that this is a story told by Plato.)

The Atlanteans prospered, but prosperity always comes before a fall and, soon enough, the gods became offended. And so the disasters started. Plato tells us that the entire island was consumed by earthquakes, sinking into the sea within two days.

BUILD CHARACTERS WITH DISTINCTIVE VOICES

1. LEFT BEHIND Think about the day the army sets out to conquer the mainland. Choose one of the following: the general, a soldier, a camp follower. Write a piece using the voice of the person they're leaving behind.

2. EUROPEAN INVASION The Atlanteans arrive in Europe. Write about this moment from the perspective of one of your characters in both the first person present tense and the first person past tense.

3. MILITARY STRATEGY An instruction manual for successful invasion: try writing the general's strategy.

4. HOW THE MIGHTY FALL Decadence! The Atlanteans become too rich. Use the following words to construct a short narrative: incense, orangutan, mountain, spice, throne.

5. WHEN THE WATERS CAME The day the world sinks. Take four inanimate objects from an Atlantean's house, and let them describe the devastation.

This story of Atlantis a great place to think about location: somewhere that actually shifts from one element to another. It also reminds us of the fleeting nature of humankind's works. And It's a fantastic place to explore voice, because there are no set characters in the myth: you can invent your own.

KEY WORD
ANAPHORA
Repeating words or phrases
at the start of sentences:
"Slowly she lifted the lid.
Slowly she unwrapped the box.
Slowly she opened the box..."

BANNING THE BARDS

Plato's *Republic* imagines an entire city bound by strict laws. He didn't allow poets in his city.

CHAPTER FIVE

GETTING *dialogue* RIGHT

Somewhere along the line, some misguided writing instructor decreed that dialogue in fiction makes a snappy and exciting read. That same person also said that the present tense is more vivid than the past. That person needs to do more reading. The past tense is just as vivid as the present. Just because things are breathless, doesn't make them exciting.

It's the same with dialogue. It does make things more vivid. But only up to a point.

One of the most common errors I see in manuscript fiction is way, way, way (is that enough ways?) too much dialogue. Behold the following:

"Hello," she said.
"Hello!" he replied.
"How are you?" she asked.
"Well, thank you," he answered.
"Oh good," she interjected.
"What shall we do today?"

You see what I mean? Just because it's dialogue, doesn't mean it's necessarily any more vivid or exciting than straightforward prose. And note the "interjected." Yes, it's a nice word, but is it doing the job any better than a straightforward "said"?

There are many things to consider when composing dialogue in fiction. Firstly, it's not the same as dialogue in plays or movies. It's easy to fall into that trap, partly because we are so saturated with television and movies.

Another common error is exactly that: the attempt to write dialogue as if it were a movie. Lots of phrases like "Let's do this!" or "It begins now." Cue swirling music, staring into the distance, etc.

That only really works when you have the visual apparatus alongside the dialogue.

Try to avoid that kind of empty tag. Perhaps you can visualize your character saying it against a filmic backdrop. Remember, this can't be seen by your readers.

The second thing is, you don't need to put down how you think a conversation might actually happen in real life. Most conversations are strange, rambling, inconsequential things: you can start with a comment about the weather, and end up with a political fight, via your dog's health and the state of the roads. In fiction, dialogue has to be much more focused, playing its part precisely and with vigor. If you sit in a café and write down what people around you say, you'll find that it tends to meander around a subject, that it's full of non-sequiturs (when a response isn't aligned with the previous statement, i.e. replying with the time when someone asks you about the weather), and that people hesitate and repeat themselves. If you're going for realism, there is a place for this, but it's very difficult to get it absolutely right. It's better, instead, to aim for realistic-sounding dialogue that conveys information and character in a concise and precise way.

Ideally speaking, dialogue has three major functions. It should inform us about somebody's character. It can tell us about plot—but it shouldn't be too full of exposition in a way that isn't natural. And it can provide relief, or add to tension or atmosphere.

A lot happens in the subtext—it's what people don't say, what the reader can infer, that can be the most powerful of all. Many creative writing anthologies and textbooks will use an Ernest Hemingway story called "Hills Like White Elephants," in which a traumatic event is never mentioned directly, but is clearly inferred by the reader.

Let's look at a couple of (made-up) examples. Let's say I'm writing a fantasy story about a queen whose empire is under threat. I want to get some information across in a scene where she talks to one of her advisers. Here's how I might start:

"The message from the Ilonians arrived this morning," said Queen Imolda.

"What did it say?" answered Tontus, her adviser.

"That the Carynthians sent armed men to the city of Volsco three days ago."

"Then we must respond immediately," said Tontus.

"I don't think so," interrupted the queen. "We must delay. We do not have enough men, and they will be exhausted by the journey. We must train up more soldiers. The threat is too great."

There's a lot of exposition going on here. I was thinking about the armies, where they're going, what the queen might be doing. But it's flat on the page. Now that I've got the information down, I might try rewriting it with less obvious dialogue, and with more attention to gesture. Remember, too, that gestures are very important when it comes to dialogue. You can replace a "he said" tag with something like "he scratched his nose." The reader will still know who's spoken. Look at this version:

Queen Imolda was studying the message from her Ilonian allies. A campaign map was spread out on the table in front of her, and she was gently tilting the small figure of a soldier from side to side.

"Act fast." Tontus began to move the queen's soldier from the citadel to Volsco.

Imolda grabbed his wrist. "And supply the men how?" She pushed the soldier back to Carynthia.

Already there's more going on. There's the detail of the map; the suggestion that the queen is planning something (without being specific); the intervention from the general; and then Imolda's reaction, which shows she's not afraid to act.

Note also that I didn't put in "she said." There are plenty of lovely ways of writing "said": interjected, advised, warned, expostulated. These have their uses, and the world would be a much poorer place without them. But they must only be used when they are absolutely precise and when no other word will do. Ninety-nine percent of the time, you're better off using "said." You can also experiment with leaving it out and replacing it with a line of gesture or atmospheric silence. Let's do that with the passage above:

Queen Imolda was studying the message from the Ilonians. The great grandfather clock was chiming the hour, and her mastiff was skittering on the polished floor. A map was spread out in front of her, and she was gently tilting the small figure of a soldier from side to side.

"Act fast." Tontus reached out and moved the soldier from the citadel Volsco.

Imolda grabbed his wrist. Her eyes were bright, but shadowed by lack of sleep. "And supply the men how?"

Think, too, how you can compress dialogue into reported speech. You can experiment with this: you can write out a whole dialogue, to see what needs to be said and what doesn't, and then you can summarize it in a line or two. This can also help to emphasize action and narrative.

It's also helpful to think about where you shouldn't use dialogue. Don't try to explain the plot laboriously:

"Hey Mom, ever since you picked up that strange ring from that store that disappeared when you went back to find it, you've been acting all weird. Are you all right?"

Don't use it for long speeches:

"Hey Mom, I was wondering about why you're acting so strange recently. I mean, what is normal? Are we normal? Am I normal? We hold everyone to completely arbitrary standards, after all. I mean, the fact that you're levitating a foot off the ground is normal for you, right? It's just everybody else that isn't."

Don't describe things or people:

"Hey Mom, I love your cool, old-fashioned, glowing skull ring! It goes so well with your white dress and that lovely faux-diamond earring you're currently trying to eat!"

You also need to consider the situation your characters are in. How do people talk differently when they're inside their own homes? They would be more private, more intimate, compared with when they're on the bus or in a bar. They might have in-jokes, or ways of saying things that are particular to their relationship.

You also have to think about your characters: how their mood affects what they might be saying. And also, crucially, what they want out of the situation. Are they trying to persuade somebody? Or are they trying to hide something? Are they lying or telling the truth?

Over the next few pages, you'll find some stories which provide lots of room for dialogue. You'll see how Pysche makes her way through various tasks, including descending into the Underworld itself to bargain with Persephone; you'll charm the Sheriff of Nottingham with Robin Hood; and you'll persuade a god to kill one of his own. All the time, think about what people are saying, why they're saying it, and how.

CUPID and PSYCHE

The bare bones of the enchanting tale of Cupid and Psyche will be familiar to any lover of fairy tales. It has its echoes in Bluebeard and in the stories of Baba Yaga. The tale comes from a bawdy Latin novel by Lucius Apuleius, of the 2nd century CE, called *The Golden Ass,* in which the hero inadvertently becomes a donkey. I've chosen it as an example of dialogue because of the many disparate scenes between characters.

THE STORY: IN A NUTSHELL

Psyche was the most beautiful daughter of a king and queen and was worshipped instead of Venus, the goddess of love. The latter, feeling jealous, sent her son Cupid to make Psyche fall in love with something ugly.

Unfortunately, Cupid grazed himself with his own arrow, thus falling in love with Psyche.

Psyche's father asked the oracle why his daughter was not yet married and was told that she was due to marry something inhuman. Horrified, the king left Psyche in the wilderness. The West Wind snatched her away, and she woke in a beautiful house where her every need was attended to.

Every night, a man visited her but forbade her from seeing his face. Eventually, Psyche persuaded him to allow her sisters to visit; when they did, they became insanely jealous of the splendor in which she lived and demanded to know who her husband was.

So Psyche hid a lamp in her bedroom and one night revealed Cupid, waking him with a splash of oil from the lamp.

Bad idea. Cupid fled.

Venus imprisoned Cupid, then, as is customary in such tales, tested Psyche: she had to sort out several piles of beans by dawn. Fortunately, some friendly ants helped her. She then had to collect water from the river Styx and, finally, take the beauty of Proserpina, the Queen of the Underworld. Proserpina agreed to give it to her in a box, telling her not to look within it.

Of course, Psyche opened the box, and immediately fell asleep.

Meanwhile, Cupid escaped from his mother and rescued Psyche. They gave the box to Venus, who made Psyche immortal so that she could marry Cupid.

At last, a happy ending. Hooray!

TRY THESE OUT FOR DIALOGUE

1. CHOP CHOP Compose the scene where Psyche persuades Cupid to allow her sisters to visit. Then cut half the dialogue.

2. MOOD CHANGE Write the scene where Venus tells Psyche to sort the heaps of beans. First do it with Venus as persuasive. Then make her rude.

3. PERSUASION The Underworld. Write the scene where Psyche meets Proserpina. How does she persuade Proserpina to give away her beauty?

4. THE BOATMAN Charon ferries Psyche across the River Styx. But what does he say to her on the journey?

5. CHITCHAT Make a list of words you associate with the king, Venus, Psyche, Cupid, and Proserpina. Then write a short piece of dialogue between any two of them at a point in the story of your choice.

KEY WORD
MONOLOGUE
Speaking on
your own.

HEART FLUTTERS
Psyche is also the Greek word for "soul" and "butterfly."

ROBIN HOOD

Everybody's favorite medieval outlaw, Robin Hood remains a compelling figure even today. He's most often thought of as an outlaw, robbing from the rich to give to the poor. As with most folktales, the version that's come down to us is a hodgepodge; many retellings make him a displaced aristocrat, whereas in the first version he's very clearly a yeoman (and the tale is set before the time of John and Richard I, the kings with whom he's most associated). Below, however, is the most common version of the story.

THE STORY: IN A NUTSHELL

Robin Hood lived in the greenwood with a band of followers known as the Merry Men. Richard the Lionheart was away fighting in the Crusades, leaving John and the barons to oppress the poor in his absence.

Robin and his band were outlaws, not paying their taxes, and robbing from the rich (and redistributing it to the poor). They dressed in green and lived in the woods and usually included the jolly, fat Friar Tuck, Little John (the giant), Alan-a-Dale the bard, and Will Scarlet, as well as Maid Marian.

One day, the Sheriff of Nottingham offered a prize of a silver arrow for the best archer at the fair. Robin decided to go, despite knowing that it was likely to be a trap.

The day arrived. Three archers appeared to undergo the contest. One, a Frenchman, a servant of the dastardly Guy of Gisborne; the second, a local Englishman; and the third, an old man in a ragged cloak. This made the dastardly Sheriff happy, as he thought Robin had been too cowardly to enter the contest.

The Frenchman shot, and missed; the local man shot, and grazed the target; the old man shot, and split the target in two. The crowd gasped: how could he show such strength?

The old man revealed himself as Robin Hood and bounded up to the Sheriff of Nottingham, snatching the silver arrow, before running back through the crowd. He and his men escaped by the skin of their teeth and jumped onto horses waiting for them outside the gates, riding off into legend.

EXPLORE THE ROLE OF DIALOGUE IN DIFFERENT INTERACTIONS

1. INCITING INCIDENT Write the scene where the outlaws learn of the contest. Make Maid Marian the voice of reason. Choose one of these as a messenger: a young girl, a talking raven, a blind man.

2. ON THE SIDELINES Write the story of the contest using dialogue between two spectators. Only use dialogue in the scene.

3. MIRROR, MIRROR What is the Sheriff of Nottingham saying? Imagine him plotting the trick. Is he perhaps talking to himself while looking in the mirror?

4. SOMETHING OLD, SOMETHING NEW Write the scene where Robin arrives back home in the greenwood, first using archaic dialogue, and then modern.

5. TONGUE-TIED Write a scene without using any dialogue whatsoever: try to convey meaning by gesture alone.

SILVER SCREEN
There have been over 100 movies of Robin Hood.

SPRING GODDESS
Maid Marian was associated with May Day celebrations.

LOKI and BALDUR

Loki is a trickster (just like Soongoo'ra the hare). He is (unlike Soongoo'ra) also the father of monsters: Hel, the world serpent Jörmungandr, and the wolf Fenrir, whom we'll meet later on at the end of the world. He's also the mother of the horse Sleipnir (he once took the form of a mare). He's slippery and mercurial: fascinating for storytellers and listeners alike. In this story, he performs one of his worst deeds. I've chosen it for dialogue because of the possibilities it offers: Asgard, the home of the gods; the gloom of the Underworld; and the entire world and its inhabitants, as Freya travels across it.

THE STORY: IN A NUTSHELL

Baldur was the most beautiful of all the Norse gods, but he became troubled by prophetic dreams. Odin, Baldur's father, rode to the Underworld in disguise to visit a prophetess. He found her in the middle of preparing a great feast. She told him that the feast was for Baldur. When Odin returned to Asgard, where the gods lived (crossing the rainbow bridge), he told Freya, Baldur's mother, what had happened; so she traveled across the universe asking everything to swear an oath not to harm Baldur.

For a while, it became a favorite game of the gods: they would hurl weapons, creatures, and other objects at Baldur, which would bounce off harmlessly. But Loki was watching. Loki crept up to Freya one day, and asked her if it was really true that everything in the whole universe had sworn an oath not

to harm Baldur. "Oh, yes," answered Freya. "It is true. Everything did. Except for one thing." "One thing?" asked Loki artlessly. "And what was that?" "Mistletoe. It's such a harmless thing, there seemed no point." She smiled at him, and went on her way.

Loki snuck away and fashioned a spear from mistletoe. He approached the blind god, Hodr, and said: "How annoying for you not to be able to join in all the fun! Here, you can throw this spear at him. I'll guide your hand!"

Hodr threw the spear. The universe watched in horror. The spear pierced Baldur, and the most beautiful of all the gods fell to his knees, clutching his throat, and died. As the rest of the gods crowded round the corpse, Loki slipped away, a sneer on his lips. The world grew darker that day.

USE THESE PROMPTS TO EXPLORE THE POSSIBILITIES OF DIALOGUE

1. OMENS Write the dialogue between Odin and the prophetess, conveying Odin's fear and the prophetess's warnings.

2. PERSUASION Pick three objects: oak tree, crab, volcano, rabbit, giant squid, Venus flytrap. Now imagine the scene where Freya has to persuade each one not to harm Loki.

3. TEMPTATION Choose Loki's words carefully. How can he make sure that the blind god will do what he says? Try two speeches: one, direct; one, round-about.

4. CONSTERNATION Write the dialogue between Odin and Loki after Baldur has died.

5. MYTH IT UP! What if Baldur is reborn and the whole story is shifted to the 21st century? How would Freya convince a computer not to kill Baldur?

KEY WORD
DICTION
The tone of dialogue, from high to low. "Good morrow, good sir," as opposed to "Howdy!"

HEXAPOD
Odin's horse, Sleipnir, has six legs.

ANTI-AGING TIPS
The Norse gods are not immortal: they are kept alive by eating magical apples.

CHAPTER SIX

PLOT and SUSPENSE

What is plot? We think of plotters as people who meet up to plan their conspiracies. Planning is an inextricable part of plot. Plot and story are not the same thing. The novelist E. M. Forster made the distinction: "The king died and then the queen died" is a story. But "The king died and then the queen died of grief" is a plot. The difference between the two is that the latter suggests a cause; in the first, the king's death might not have had any bearing on the queen at all.

A plot, that series of events, must have a sense of necessity: a strong pull onward, forcing you to continue until you reach the end where everything is satisfactorily resolved–or not.

We read for many reasons: to enjoy the beauty of language and to experience new worlds, but also because we want to know what will happen to a set of characters and their problems. Will Achilles' anger abate? Will Hamlet avenge his father? Will Harry Potter kill Voldemort? Will Elizabeth Bennet marry Darcy? That's the crucial component: the force that pushes you on. All literature, great and minor, can be resolved into one single question in this way.

Plots also have a psychological function: they tell you something about your own mind as well as about the world. We want meaning from stories: this helps us to understand our place in the world and how we act within it.

There are many theories about how many plots, and how many kinds of plots, exist. Thriller writer John Gardner once said that there are only two kinds: a man goes on a journey or a stranger comes to town. In the first, the hero, in journeying, develops into a different kind of character; in the second, the town is disrupted by the new arrival and must adjust itself. This can also be seen if you categorize plots as "siege narratives" or "quest narratives." Either the plot is, essentially, about someone dealing with outside pressures; or the hero is going out on a quest. When you come to your own story, ask yourself: is your protagonist acting or reacting?

If you look online, you may find yourself confused by how many different kinds of plot structures there are. I think the most helpful is journalist Christopher Booker's analysis: that there are seven basic plots.

THE SEVEN PLOT STRUCTURES:

1. RAGS TO RICHES
The obvious example of this is Cinderella, or many fairy tales in which the miller's son becomes the prince. You can also think about it as moving from a state of emotional rags to emotional riches.

2. OVERCOMING THE MONSTER
The classic, archetypal myths feature these heavily. There's a dragon devastating the land: call on the hero to kill it! Again, the monster can be a psychological one, or an antagonist of some kind.

3. QUEST
There's a magical sword in the highest caves of the northern mountains! You need to get it to save your village! Go! Again, the quest can be transferred to a modern setting very easily—it can be finding a lost relative or solving a crime.

4. VOYAGE AND RETURN
This is different from the above, as the return element is crucial to the movement of the plot. Think of the *Odyssey*, for example: Odysseus has to get home—his return is the end of the plot.

5. COMEDY
This doesn't just mean an episode of *Friends*. It means that you start with a disordered situation and then move toward order. This usually lends itself to laughter and is often set in a contemporary situation.

6. TRAGEDY
The opposite of comedy: tragedy begins with order and moves toward disorder. This can mean terrible events piling up, and plenty of deaths.

7. REBIRTH
The protagonist begins the story with negative traits and is then reborn through the process of the plot. *A Christmas Carol*, in which Scrooge is reborn through his adventures with the three ghosts, is a good example.

Once you've thought about which kind of plot you want to use, you can then think about structuring it. There are many different kinds of structures, but the most useful is one used in screenwriting: three acts. Each section of the plot moves toward a particular point.

-Act I -
Setup
Exposition, Inciting Incident,
Plot Point One

-Act II -
Confrontation
Rising Action, Midpoint,
Plot Point Two

-Act III -
Resolution
Pre-Climax, Climax,
Denouement

It looks so easy like that, doesn't it? When you set out your plot points, you can try to fit them into this structure. Don't worry if they don't fit exactly—they're only structures and are there to be played around with.

Each moment in the plot has to reach forward toward the next. Your character makes a decision: we need to know what will happen if your character doesn't make that particular decision. Another useful term is "the stakes." What is at stake? If Anna doesn't pick up the phone and call her boss, will she get fired? And if she does, will she get that promotion she's always wanted? Either way will push her into a new place. If Femi doesn't go to the school dance, will he lose his best friend? Or will he go and have the best night of his life?

A lot of the fun in fiction comes from raising the stakes, which helps to create suspense. Suspense doesn't have to mean ratcheting things up so that you're constantly biting your nails; it can also be a more gentle movement. But it does help to imagine a clock gently ticking.

One way to think about it is that you must put obstacles in the way of your protagonist. There are plenty of fun exercises you can do to help with this. Let's say that your protagonist, Jean-Pierre, wants to get to school on time so he can finish his art project, which is due that day. But what if... the car breaks down. So he takes the bus. The bus gets diverted. So he gets out and runs. It starts raining, so he's soaking wet. He trips, and loses a shoe ... he arrives, dripping wet, only to find that the school gates have closed and he's not allowed in any more... He watches through the window as everyone else lines up to hand in their portfolios.

As a result of this, Jean-Pierre gets an extra lesson with his art teacher. Also in the lesson is a beautiful new pupil... soon he falls in love, and, with the help of his new amour, goes on to produce better art than he ever had before. As a result of this... And so on.

This goes for any kind of plot structure. If you're on a mission to get supplies from Base 247 in Crater A432 because your camp has run out of spare oxygen, then what if your buggy loses energy? What if your tracker breaks? What if, what if, what if... always keep asking yourself that crucial question.

The other thing, however, is to always test for plausibility. If your heroine wakes up in bed one morning and her mother is missing, she's not necessarily going to sit down and have some cornflakes. Think about what is psychologically and logically plausible. Reactions and results have to fit within the framework of your narrative. That means establishing rules and boundaries. If you're writing in a magical world, you need to be aware of the rules. If your protagonist can simply solve everything by wishing or waving a wand, then it takes all the tension out of a story. J. K. Rowling deals with this very well, as the spells her wizards learn have limits, and can be wrongly applied.

Another technique that's great for suspense is dramatic irony. If your reader knows something that your character doesn't, it can work really well. One other thing to try is to mix up the chronological sequence. We think in chronological order, and we tend to tell stories in chronological order: but consider how you can use flashbacks and flashforwards effectively to create suspense. Sometimes, starting with the end result of a scenario can urge the reader onward to find out how we got there (flashforward). Sometimes, a flashback can help to contextualize or contrast with what's going on in the present time of the narrative.

Remember: Don't give everything away all at once. Hold things back from the reader. Tease things out, step by step. And then, gradually, lead up to your devastating climax.

BANG!

CUCHULAINN'S DEATH

The Irish legend of Cuchulainn is up there with Achilles and King Arthur. The story around his death is perfectly plotted: every element slots beautifully into place, with even minor details like the raven and the sword having a crucial role to play. Cuchulainn is under a spell that means he is unable to eat the flesh of a hound; this proves important, too. Note how nothing is wasted. Even Lugaid has a reason for killing Cuchulainn: revenge. Following every thread of a legend can lead you down many avenues.

THE STORY: IN A NUTSHELL

Cuchulainn was the champion of Ulster, and he killed anyone who challenged him. One day, he slew Calatan the sorceror, whose pregnant wife gave birth to two sets of triplets. They were brought up with revenge burning in their hearts.

When the King of Ulster heard of their plan to kill Cuchulainn, he tried to protect his best fighter for as long as he could. The children of Calatan came to Ulster and created a magical battle outside to entice Cuchulainn out to fight.

The king called for a great feast, and the sounds of cheer covered up the magical noises. This went on for three days and three nights until the king realized he couldn't keep up the feasting any longer (think of the expense!), and transported Cuchulainn to

the Valley of the Deaf where no sound from outside could intrude.

The children of Calatan did not demur. One of the daughters entered the camp disguised as Niamh, a friend of Cuchulainn's, and told him he was needed to fight. Cuchulainn tried to hitch up his horse; three times the horse shied away, until Cuchulainn succeeded. Then the horse wept tears of blood. (Remember Achilles' magical horses? Same kind of deal.)

More omens occurred along the way: he stumbled across three old women feasting on a hound, who bade him join them; he refused. But they insisted, and as soon as a morsel touched his lips, he felt the strength ebb from half his body. The three old women were actually the Morrigan, the goddess of war, in disguise; she wanted her revenge on him.

Later, he came upon the three sons of Calatan, and Lugaid, the son of Cu Roi. There was a prophecy that the first three spears Cuchulainn threw would kill three kings.

The first son asked him for a spear, saying that if Cuchulainn didn't comply, he would slander Cuchulainn. Cuchulainn hurled a spear through his head. Lugaid threw it back, and it slew his charioteer, the king of charioteers.

The second son did the same, threatening to slander all of Ulster. Cuchulainn refused and killed the second son with his spear. Lugaid threw the spear back, this time killing the horse, the king of horses.

The third son also asked for the spear and threatened to slander Cuchulainn himself; Cuchulainn dispatched him in the same way. This time, when Lugaid threw the spear back, it pierced Cuchulainn in the stomach.

The hero crawled to a standing stone and tied himself to it, holding his sword; a raven tripped over his intestines. Cuchulainn died laughing—he was the third, and final, king. He remained there for three days, until the wary Morrigan turned into a raven and sat on his shoulder to see if he would move; he didn't.

Coda: Lugaid tried to get Cuchulainn's sword but was unable to wrest it free; he severed the tendon on Cuchulainn's hand, and the sword, in falling, chopped off Lugaid's hand. Lugaid then fought Conall Cernach, who sportingly tucked one hand into his belt; but Conall won and put Lugaid's head on a stone.

The stone melted.

PRACTICE SOME PLOT EXERCISES

1. IN MEDIAS RES Begin in the middle, with Cuchulainn meeting the three sons of Catalan. How does this affect the movement of the story?

2. PLOT POINTS Write out the story as a series of plot points. Change one and see what happens.

3. ACTION Choose the King of Ulster, an old woman, or Lugaid as a character. Then choose one of these three actions: "belly laughing," "swimming," or "dancing." Pick one of each at random, and then rewrite the climax with one of those actions.

4. QUEST Write your own quest for Cuchulainn based around words like jewel, goat, wizard, stream, and wine.

5. ALL IN THE MIND Choose an incident from the story of Cuchulainn. Adapt it by making the characters live today. Turn the problems into psychological ones.

6. HIDING Use the idea of Cuchulainn waiting for his horse to develop your own plot. He has an object in his luggage that he wants to conceal...

7. HEROINE Cuchulainn leaves his magical spear behind at an inn. A young girl picks it up... develop a plot from that premise.

8. DESPAIR Think about what Cuchulainn wants. Then take it away from him.

KEY WORD
FRAME NARRATIVE
A story framing
another story.

TRUE LOVE
Cuchulainn was trained by the warrior goddess Scatha, and fought Athe, the strongest woman in the world.
He married her.

the THREE APPLES

The Three Apples is an intricately plotted narrative, full of twists and turns. It comes from the *Thousand and One Nights*, the series of stories that wise and beautiful Scheherazade tells her husband, the Sultan, in order to stay alive. He has a habit of killing his wives, you see, so she must keep him entertained. Think about how you can introduce surprises into your writing and pull that metaphorical rug from underneath your reader.

THE STORY: IN A NUTSHELL

A fisherman found a locked chest in the Tigris river and sold it to the Caliph. Inside were the remains of a young woman. The Caliph ordered his vizier to solve the crime within three days or be executed. The vizier failed and was about to be killed when two men appeared, both claiming to be the murderer. One was young and handsome, the other an old man. Each claimed the other was a liar. Eventually, the young one proved that he was the murderer by describing the chest. He was the woman's husband and the old man was her father trying to save his son-in-law.

The young man said that she had been a brilliant wife and mother. One day she had asked for a rare apple, as she was ill. He journeyed to Basra and found three apples. On his return, his wife refused to eat them. Later, he discovered a slave carrying one of the apples, and the slave told him that his girlfriend had given it to him after her husband had given the apples to her. It was

devastating. He rushed home, found one of the apples missing, and killed his wife. He then threw the box into the river.

When he returned, his own son said he had stolen one of the apples and the slave had run off with it. Distraught, the young man demanded to be executed. The Caliph refused and set the vizier a task: he must find the slave within three days or be executed.

Unable to find the slave, the vizier was summoned for execution. He said goodbye to his family and hugged his daughter. In her pocket was an apple; the name of the Caliph was written on it. She told her father that she had bought it from their slave. The final twist: the culprit was the vizier's own slave. The vizier begged the Caliph to forgive the slave and told him a story in compensation. The Caliph enjoyed the story, pardoned the slave, and provided a new wife for the young man. Everybody was happy—except for the murdered woman...

TRY SOME MORE PROMPTS FOR PLOT

1. TEMPLATE Write down the plot points for the story of The Three Apples, including the framing device. Now use this as a basis to write your own version.

2. THREE ACTS Can you fit the story into three acts? What do you have to change or alter to make it fit?

3. FLASHBACK/FLASHFORWARD Try writing the story using flashbacks or flashforwards.

4. SURPRISE Plot out a different ending in which the wife was alive the whole time.

5. MYTH IT UP! Give the wife a name and make her kill the husband. How does this alter the plot?

KEY WORD
CLIMAX
The point at which
the story reaches
its height.

KEY WORD
DENOUEMENT
The moment when
everything is revealed.

OEDIPUS

One of the best-known stories in all of Greek myth, this narrative builds to its excruciating climax with one of the greatest devices ever known in drama: Oedipus is trying to find out who killed his father, as a plague is attacking his city, and a priest has warned him that he must purge the city of the killer in order to divert the plague. As a plot, it's supreme, deftly using dramatic irony in a harrowing manner and inching toward the inevitable and devastating end.

THE STORY: IN A NUTSHELL

There was a prophecy, as there nearly always is: Oedipus, brought up in Corinth by people he thought were his parents, learned from the oracle at Delphi that he was fated to kill his father and marry his mother. So, sensibly, he decided to leave home and go on his travels. Along the way, at a crossroads, he got into a quarrel with a fellow traveler and killed him. On reaching the city of Thebes, he ran into the Sphinx, a monster who was terrorizing the land; if he couldn't answer her riddle, she would eat him. Oedipus answered the riddle successfully and entered Thebes to find that the city's king, Laius, had been killed; he married the queen, and ruled well.

Many years later, a ravaging plague brought an answer from the oracle: he must find out who killed Laius, and then the city would be purified. So, step by step, Oedipus inquired into the events of the day, and, slowly but surely, uncovered the terrible truth: the man who killed Laius was himself. He had not only murdered his own father, but married his mother and had children with her. Oedipus blinded himself, and wandered, an outcast, for the rest of his life.

EXPLORE THE ENDLESS POSSIBILITIES OF PLOT

1. WHAT IF... The plot of Oedipus is relentless: the frame narrative of the prophecy that cannot be escaped; the Sphinx that must be overcome; the plague which must be quelled: every question, every new witness that Oedipus calls, serves to move the plot onward in only one direction—toward the truth. It seems almost sacrilegious to tamper with it. And yet... what if Oedipus still refused to understand? What if he blamed someone else and carried on ruling? Write a scene where the plague ravages the city, and the self-deluding king sits among the ruins.

2. DEAR DIARY Write a diary entry from the point of view of one of the following: the Sphinx, the queen, or the prophet.

3. GENDER SWAPS The Oedipus complex is often thought of in tandem with that of Electra. Can you try gender-swapping the roles so that a girl accidentally kills her mother and marries her father?

4. THE RELUCTANT HERO What if Oedipus decided that he would stay in Corinth? The prophecy had to be fulfilled: how would circumstances bring his real mother and father to him?

5. RIDDLE ME THIS Try writing riddles to trap your characters. The riddle given to Oedipus goes as follows: What is that which in the morning goeth upon four feet; upon two feet in the afternoon; and in the Evening upon three?

KEY WORD
RISING ACTION
What happens before the
main action happens.

LEG-ENDARY
Oedipus is supposed to mean "swollen foot."

CHAPTER SEVEN

METAMORPHOSIS

Metamorphosis, or transformation, is an essential part of any narrative. In fact, you could argue that it's the thing that holds everything together. (Which is odd, when you think about it.)

Scenes change, allowing you to contrast one place with another. The plot moves onward, from one changing situation to another, creating tension and excitement. As the plot moves, the characters change, becoming stronger or weaker, or better at table tennis or worse at parenting.

And as we read, we grow and we change, too. That's partly why the Harry Potter series is so successful. Unlike, say, Enid Blyton's Famous Five series, where the children are locked into an eternal childhood, Harry Potter grew and struggled up the ranks of his school in the same way his readers did.

As we live, we grow, too, and our perceptions change. We finish the best stories looking at the world around us with brand-new eyes. That is the magic and power of writing. That is why we all do it, and hope to do it as best we can.

All novels will demonstrate this process of change. There's a particular type of novel, for example, called a bildungsroman, which is about the growth of a youth into an adult. This is often based around an epiphany in which the character realizes something that forces them to change.

There are several different types of metamorphosis. In literal form, it brings wonder and delight to the plot. We all love stories in which people turn into animals, and it's been a feature of fiction since time began—think of Odysseus' men turning into pigs.

Literally putting people into a different skin is a fabulous way of exploring their characters.

C. S. Lewis, in *The Voyage of the Dawn Treader*, has the greedy, unpleasant Eustace Stubbs turn into a dragon; in this form he experiences what it feels like to be alienated, and he learns to change his ways. Alice, in *Alice in Wonderland* by Lewis Carroll, grows bigger and smaller, thus experiencing what it feels like to grow up.

In Greek mythology it's common to be turned into a tree by a god or goddess.

It's not just in children's literature: Franz Kafka's short story *The Metamorphosis* has one of the best first lines in all fiction: "As Gregor Samsa awoke one morning from uneasy dreams, he found himself transformed in his bed into an enormous insect." This allows the writer to explore some very difficult themes of family and isolation. In Keats's poem, "Lamia," a man marries a woman, only for her to turn out to have been a snake. Beauty and the Beast, the aforementioned sailors in the *Odyssey*... everywhere you look, there are people turning into beasts, and, sometimes, back again. The common thread between all of these is wonder.

One of the most compelling long narratives in all literature is Ovid's poem, the *Metamorphoses*. Ovid was a Roman poet writing in the age of the Emperor Augustus (in the 1st century CE), and his poem, at the time, was strikingly new and daring. It didn't deal with just one subject or hero, unlike previous epic poems (like the *Iliad*, which focuses on Achilles), but instead presented a dazzling array of stories, all interconnecting and joining and reflecting each other.

Many of the stories see people changing into animals or birds. There is Lycaon, punished for his sinfulness by becoming a wolf. You may have heard of Arachne, turning into a spider, or Daphne, becoming a laurel wreath. There are hundreds of others: people become streams, stags, flowers, gods, nymphs, birds, stones, spiders, constellations, lizards, snakes, bears, seals, cattle, swans, trees, even a dog and a weasel. Each one has its own resonance and significance. And each one is ripe for adaptation.

THE UNIVERSE IS OPEN

The whole universe is open for exploration, and the possibilities for literal metamorphoses are endless. Your characters could change into robots, aliens, ants, paper clips... well, maybe not paper clips. You get the picture.

Transformation, too, works on a narrative level. Take a genre: school stories. Then put the school on a rocket going to Mars. What about pony stories? Give the ponies wings and make them talk. Has that happened before? Then make one of them a gangster and one of them a cowboy. Anything you can do to play with established narratives is great.

Magical narratives take what's normal and make it strange: think of the Hogwarts Express in J. K. Rowling's Harry Potter series: a steam train, torn from its context, becomes a wondrous mode of transportation. Think, too, how you can achieve that with the ordinary things around you. Your pen: could it write the future? Your ring: if you turned it, could it make you talk to animals?

Really, that is what the best narratives are all about: the ordinary made extraordinary, the mundane made marvelous. The best writers can make you look anew at a cloud or a stone; they can transform the way you think about and perceive the world.

REASONS, REASONS

With human transformations, the first thing that you need to think about is: why? Why have your character change into a wolf? Or a robot? Or a ship? Or a rock? Does the transformation emotionally reflect some aspect of the character? Does it fit in with the themes and the narrative logic? It makes sense for Eustace to turn into a dragon, because that is a world in which dragons exist; it wouldn't make much sense for Alice to turn into one, as her narrative doesn't allow for it.
(The Jabberwocky exists in a poem within the story—but doesn't encroach on the story itself.)

Then consider what your protagonist can learn while in that form. Is it a punishment or a reward? In E. Nesbit's *Five Children and It*, the children grow wings when they wish for flight; but they soon discover that it isn't all it's cracked up to be.

When endowing objects with magical powers, consider carefully the consequences. Chris Priestley's brilliant series of short stories, *Uncle Montague's Tales of Terror*, are full of magical objects: a mirror that seems to entice you to sin, for example. In that story, the mirror is a way of showing how the self can be deceptive. The ring of power, in Tolkien's *Lord of the Rings*, is a symbol too: it's something that unites all the other rings, and it's also handily portable. (Think how the story would have been different had it been a magical sword or shield.)

As with everything we've been talking about so far, it is important to have a sense of the consequences and resonances of things.

The story in this chapter hinges on transformations. The selkies' beautiful tales are told all over Scotland. Use this story to work on atmosphere, dialogue, setting, and, above all, transformation, both literal and emotional.

the SELKIE WIFE

The poignant selkie story is full of longing and love. The metamorphosis here perhaps speaks of the ways that people need to change themselves for marriage; it perhaps also says something about the relations between men and women. The child in this story is particularly moving: the youngest making the decision that his mother should return to her native element. Use the story to play with the idea of metamorphosis, and see if you can link it to emotional or atmospheric change.

THE STORY: IN A NUTSHELL

One day, after an unsuccessful trip out to sea, a fisherman noticed the selkie people playing on the shore. They did not see him, and he watched them in wonder. A sealskin was lying on the rocks, and he picked it up, thinking that nobody would believe him unless he showed it to them. As he turned to go, he heard wailing. A beautiful woman rushed up to him. "You must give me my skin back," she said. "I cannot return to my people without it." But the fisherman had already fallen in love with her. "Come with me, and be my wife," he said. Greatly saddened, the selkie woman followed him to his cottage where he looked after her and brought her fresh fish. He hid her skin in the chimney, hoping that she would never find it. The selkie woman would gaze at the sea and sing mournful songs that spoke of the waves. In time, however, she grew to love the gentle fisherman. They had seven children together. But the woman would wander out to the shoreline and gaze at the sea.

One day, the fisherman was out in the boat with three of the children; three others had gone to the village for bread. The selkie woman and the seventh child were left alone together. She was looking out of the window at the shore, as always. "Why are you so sad, mother?" asked the youngest child.

The selkie woman did not reply, but the child saw the seals, and, knowing of the legend of the selkies, ran to the chimney and pulled out the sealskin. "I saw father looking at this, and I knew it was important," she said. The selkie woman took the skin and joyfully ran down to the shoreline.

When the fisherman returned, he noticed a female seal gazing at him for a moment before she disappeared. He never saw her again. And although the fisherman was saddened by this, he knew his young child had done the right thing, and that his wife was much happier in the salt waves among her own people.

WRITE YOUR OWN MAGICAL TRANSFORMATIONS

1. TRANSFORMATION Describe the transformation from seal to woman, focusing entirely on the senses.

2. AND AGAIN Now write the transformation from the point of view of the watching fisherman.

3. AND AGAIN Now write it back from woman to seal. How are things different?

4. WHAT IF THEY WEREN'T SEALS? Choose from one of the following animals: bear, swan, deer, dog, red panda, iguana, emu, platypus, spider... Shift the setting, too.

5. MYTH IT UP! Try different endings—what if the father and the children decided to become selkies too?

KEY WORD
EPIPHANY
An event that causes a character to realize something important.

KEY WORD
BILDUNGSROMAN
A novel about a young
person growing into
an adult.

FOLK MEMORIES
Some people think selkies are folk memories of sealskin-wearing peoples.

CHAPTER EIGHT

ENDINGS

We all know what makes a good ending. We also all know when an ending is completely unsatisfactory and leaves you hurling a book across a room, or shouting in horror at your screen, or shaking your head as you walk home from the bus with your audiobook on.

It's something that unites people: that need for a satisfying conclusion is universal.

All the way through your writing, you've been making decisions: about where your characters should go, why they go there, and what they do when they're there.

Now we must see the end result of those decisions. The balloon that went up at the beginning is coming down.

You've seen how your plot must have movement. You've seen how your protagonist, endowed with qualities, quirks, and flaws, will push onward.

The tests have been passed. The villains have been defeated. Your characters' goals have been achieved (we hope). The ring has been found and destroyed. The monster has been slain. The wedding is approaching. Your character has faced the crisis and succeeded; and now will return home, having gained extra knowledge or skills, and having healed or saved the world. Or done their history project. Or won their football match against their rival. Or lost their football match.

There is a real feeling of joy—and of release, too.

Whereas the beginning of a story tells you that you're about to enter into a fictional world—what some people might call the Storyworld—the ending reminds us that reality exists once more, and we must return to it. The fairy, Puck, at the end of Shakespeare's play *A Midsummer Night's Dream*, reminds us all that we are watching a fiction. Curtains close, lights go up, and everybody wipes their eyes and goes home for a nice supper.

Both excitement and sadness are associated with an ending. A beginning creates an expectation, which, with luck, the middle of your work explores; the ending then fulfills that expectation.

Sometimes this can have a moral purpose. In a crime fiction, you want the murderer to be found and punished. Other endings have different purposes, but we still feel their rightness: the lovers get married (or stay together); the king is avenged; the city is built; the lost dog is found. A happy ending, where everything becomes ordered, gives us hope; a tragic ending, with everything in chaos, reminds us of the precariousness of life.

What we look for is both closure and resolution (unless, of course, you are playing a narrative game and want things to remain unresolved. But there's plenty of time for that).

We know what the end of a piece of string looks like. The end of the road, the end of the affair... but how do you transfer this certain knowledge—that things are finite, that everything has a conclusion—to your plot and your story, so that your ending is both satisfying and surprising? How do you avoid a stereotypical ending, while at the same time working within the particular limits of your narrative?

There are many things that you should avoid when you're ending your work. "It was all a dream..." should certainly be avoided. This only works if the dream then has an effect, demonstrably, upon the character or circumstances of the person who dreamed it. Otherwise, it's

an odd trick to play on your readers. Fiction is meant to bring us into a believable fictional world: so why then tell us that the story we've just read is not even a coherent part of the fictional world?

You should also try to avoid predictable endings. Now, of course, the killer must be found; the monster must be killed; the couple must get together. But it's how they get there that provides the pitfalls. Think of the brilliant movie *Toy Story 3*, where right up until the very end we are led to believe that the toys will be destroyed... and then... well, you'll just have to watch it.

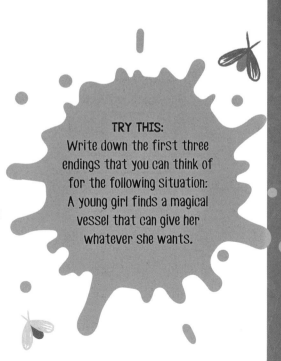

TRY THIS:
Write down the first three endings that you can think of for the following situation: A young girl finds a magical vessel that can give her whatever she wants.

TRY THIS:
Think about the endings of your three favorite books. How do they respond to the beginnings? How do they both frustrate and satisfy expectations?

Endings must suit the genre you're writing in. It's no good ending your hilarious romcom with a triple murder (unless you're making a different sort of statement). It's no good ending your zombie apocalypse horror with everyone making friends (ditto).

Endings must be suggested, hinted at, foreshadowed. The shape of the story needs it. Endings remain in your mind (like beginnings). We think about them more than the middle parts. That's why they've got to resonate properly. Your endings, then, must be suitable for the logic of the narrative. They must be plausible, and fit in with what's gone before. They have to make you sit up in surprise, but they must also seem inevitable. One of my favorite endings is in the play *Medea,* by Euripides. In it, Medea kills her children (she has reasons); and then, instead of being punished, she flies off in a chariot drawn by dragons. It works so well because, although we know that Medea is planning to leave for Athens,

we have no idea how she will get there (and whether she will be allowed to go); it also reminds us that she is a powerful witch and granddaughter of the sun god. Surprise! Another of my favorites can be found in Shakespeare's *Hamlet.* There, Hamlet gets his revenge on Claudius (though he didn't really want it in the first place); and the bodies pile up. The young Fortinbras, a minor character, comes onstage: but what does he bring with him? The promise of a new, better political order, or simply more of the same?

The wolf Fenrir, brother to Jörmungandr, is part of the story of Ragnarök.

ENDINGS AND BEGINNINGS

The ending of George Eliot's *The Mill on the Floss* has me in tears every single time I read it. When I watch the 1980s fantasy movie *The Princess Bride*, the ending leaves me delighted every single time, even though I must have watched it so many times now that I can quote almost every line. With your ending, you have the wonderful opportunity for your story to linger in someone's mind forever.

Some people know the endings of their books before they've even started writing: an image, a line, something that's bothering them. Then they go back to the start and see what events might lead up to that point. Others don't have any idea and see where the characters take them.

You don't have to do either one or the other: you can decide and develop in your own way. Just remember to think about plausibility.

And the great thing about endings is that an ending invokes both its own beginning–and new ones.

So, we're coming to the end of this little book. I hope you've enjoyed reading the prompts and the stories, and I hope you've had fun making your own.

In the following stories we'll return to the richness and strangeness of Norse myth, where they really did like their endings; and we'll have a look at the compelling idea of Bigfoot and wild men in general.

Now go forth, and create some brilliant endings!

Artemis, the Greek goddess of the hunt is the daughter of Zeus and the twin sister of Apollo. Diana is her Roman counterpart, as Jupiter is for Zeus.

THOR and the WORLD SERPENT

This tumultuous story from Norse mythology is about endings.
It is also about the beginning of the end...

THE STORY: IN A NUTSHELL

Thor and the World Serpent, Jörmungandr, were enemies from the moment the snake was born and thrown by Odin into the sea, where it grew and grew until it encircled the whole Earth, grasping its own tail.

Three times Thor was to encounter the World Serpent. The first time, a giant transformed the snake into a cat and asked Thor to lift it. Not knowing the cat was really the World Serpent, Thor struggled and struggled, until he managed to shift just one paw. The giant said that this was fortunate, though, as he transformed it back and stretched it out until it reached the sky: if Thor had been able to lift the whole thing, he would have changed the whole universe.

The second time, Thor was on a fishing trip with another giant. This giant refused to give Thor any bait, so Thor, in a rage, chopped off the head of one of the giant's oxen and used that. The World Serpent took the bait, and Thor dragged him up. Imagine the scene: the enormous, scaly head, vaster than a mountain, heaving up from the sea, its fangs longer than trees, its eyes like boulders. Thor was about to smash the serpent with his hammer when the giant cut the fishing line and it sank back to the bottom of the seabed, leaving nary a ripple.

The third time was the start of the end of everything. One of the signs of Ragnarök, the end of the world, was the violence and storms of the seas, and so the world serpent finally slithered out onto dry land, seeking his brother Fenrir, the wolf (see page 168 for Fenrir's part in Ragnarök).

Thor must battle Jörmungandr to save the world. And so he and the mountainous creature face off one last time. Their battle went on for days as the world collapsed around them. And in the end, there was little point: the world was going to end anyway. Thor, with one mighty blow of his hammer, slew the serpent; and then, walking away, he managed to stagger nine steps before falling to the ground himself. The god was dead.

EXPLORE SOME DIFFERENT ENDINGS

1. FORESHADOWING The World Serpent meets Thor three times. Describe the first time they meet from the serpent's perspective. Try to foreshadow the ending.

2. HAMMER IT OUT Give Thor's hammer sentience. How does it feel about the end of the world? How does it talk?

3. LAND AND SEA The creatures on land will be invaded by those of the sea. Write a four-paragraph description from the point of view of a Viking girl watching from a tree top.

4. DEATH OF A GOD It's unexpected; it's poignant. Describe the battle between the world serpent, Jörmungandr and Thor, emphasizing the loss of the god through emotional and physical detail.

5. MYTH IT UP! You can do anything you want! What gods can you bring in from other pantheons? Could Apollo be called in to help? Or perhaps the Egyptian gods? Or gods of your own invention?

DOES WHAT IT SAYS
ON THE TIN
Jörmungandr, the World
Serpent, means "Huge
Monster." He eats his own
tail: the ouroboros.

KEY WORD
PAYOFF
The punchline. In a short story, this will be a line or symbol that relates back to the beginning.

KEY WORD
CLIFFHANGER
An ending that leaves
its plot unresolved.

BIGFOOT

Bigfoot appears in the Endings section, as there isn't really any one particular story, the idea of a wild, hairy, humanlike creature that lives in the wilderness being common to many cultures. The word "bigfoot" seems to originate from the nickname for a large bear; it became conflated with the Sasquatch and the other wildmen who steal salmon and snatch away children. Wodwos and green men in England, yetis in Tibet Region of China: they are prevalent everywhere. Apply your new techniques to the idea, and then come up with your own story. Just think about how the beginning should lead to the ending. Choose your plot and off you go...

THE STORY: IN A NUTSHELL

It was meant to be an easy hunting trip. Sam and his father had been camping for two nights already, and Sam was almost used to the mosquitos, the hard ground, and the smell. But he hadn't gotten used to the darkness at night or the sounds of the wilderness all around him. They hadn't caught anything yet, but Sam didn't mind that; and nor, he thought, did his father. Instead, they enjoyed simply being with each other, not saying much, just tracking through the woods, hoping to find a deer.

The third night, it was especially dark and especially cold. Sam couldn't sleep. He pulled his sweater on, but it was no good. Perhaps he should go and sit by the fire. He edged toward the tent flap.

A shuffling sound. A grunt. Something was rummaging in their bags. He peered out. Lit by the low flames, a large shape.

His heart contracted. It was a bear. But then it did something that no bear would ever do. It stood up on its hind legs and looked from side to side, for all the world like a human. For a moment he thought it was looking straight at him. And then, it was gone.

The next morning, Sam saw that their belongings had been riffled through. Most of their food, canned and packaged, was intact. But the fresh stuff was gone. And beside the fire, a footprint. His father put his shoe down beside it. Then he put down his other shoe beside it, end to end. The footprint was as long as two men's shoes! "Sam," he said. "Get out the camera..."

The pictures of the enormous footprint made the front page of the national press, and then the international press. They hadn't caught a deer. But they'd certainly caught something—if only they knew what it was...

DISCOVER WHERE A STORY CAN TAKE YOU

1. A SERIES OF VERY UNFORTUNATE EVENTS Use the *What if...* technique to describe when a Bigfoot child goes out without its parents knowing... Make the ending reflect the beginning.

2. ATMOSPHERICS Describe the forest, using the word "isolation" as your theme.

3. CONSEQUENCES Think of the possible consequences of a Bigfoot being found. What would this mean for science?

4. PLOTTING IT OUT Use the following objects to plot out and finish a story: backpack, map, mysterious tooth, bow and arrow, teddy bear.

5. MYTH IT UP! Write a letter to a Bigfoot thanking him or her for something they did that helped you.

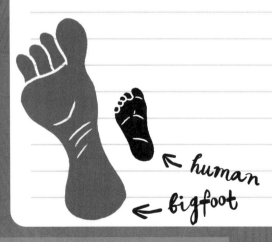

← human

← bigfoot

RAGNARÖK

It is fitting to end this book with a story about the end of the entire universe. Ragnarök is one of the most troubling of all myths because it tells us that the gods can die, and that the universe can be destroyed. As an ending, it can't be beaten, really. Yet, it does contain within it a seed of hope... And that's why it's the final story.

THE STORY: IN A NUTSHELL

The gods knew it was coming. They always knew, from the very beginning, that their endings were folded up for them, waiting, in absolute night and nothingness. At first, the Great Winter would come—the Fimbulwinter. Heimdall would blow his horn, the sound shivering around the homes of the gods. The World Serpent would thrash and the waves roar, as the beast slunk onto land, and Thor, distracted, would go off to fight it. The shakings of the world would cause the ship, *Naglfar*, to come loose from its moorings. Made from human nails and crewed by giants, the ship would unleash chaos. Loki would be their captain. The giant Sutr, with his shining sword, would stride up from the south to fight with Freyr, and the wolf, Fenrir, would attack Odin himself, his eyes blazing.

The gods fought. They did not win. Odin died. Freyr died. Thor, as we know, died fighting the world serpent.

The Sun turned black, eaten at last by Fenrir, who had chased it for eternity. The Earth sank into the sea, the stars disappeared, and flames reached the heavens. There was nothing. Emptiness.

Yet some gods did survive. Ragged, torn, they met on the field at Iðavöllr (*Ith-a-voll-er*), and from the ashes they built a new city. And two humans, a man and a woman, who had hidden themselves, came forward and lived in peace and joy. A new Sun rose.

And best of all: there was a god who had long ago been killed through the tricks of Loki. A god who was the most beautiful. A god for whom the whole universe wept. Up from the depths of Hel, came Baldur.

And so in the end, there were new beginnings.

THE END OF THE WORLD...

1. FATAL BREAKFAST Have a go at writing about the morning of the beginning of the end of the world.

2. DETAILS Choose one of the following: Heimdall, the World Serpent, or Sutr. Write a really detailed description.

3. WORD ASSOCIATIONS Write down the first ten words you think of following "end."

4. MYTH IT UP! How to avoid the end—what can the gods do to stop it? Write a scene in which three gods decide to take things into their own hands.

5. OVER TO YOU We're at the end! We've done it! And now, I pass the baton on to you, dear writer-friend. Take your pen, and write what you wish...

KEY WORD
CLOSURE
When a narrative
resolves a conflict.

KEY WORD
EPILOGUE
This can often
look toward a
direct sequel.

THEY HAD IT COMING
The word Ragnarök means
"fate of the gods."

DEATH OF THE GODS?
Some say the Ragnarök
story represents the death
of belief in the gods, thanks
to the coming of Christ.

MORE STORIES TO INSPIRE

HERE'S A SELECTION OF SYNOPSES OF OTHER FANTASTIC TALES. THESE ARE ALL STORIES THAT HAVE ATTAINED A "MYTH-LIKE" STATUS THAT I WOULD HAVE LOVED TO INCLUDE. USE THEM AS A SPRINGBOARD FOR YOUR IMAGINATION.

ANANSI AND THE SKY GOD'S STORIES

The trickster Anansi wants to buy the Sky God's stories. He can't have them, except for the price of a python, a leopard, a fairy, and a hornet. Using his cunning, Anansi captures them all, and wins the stories.

BETUSHKA AND THE GOLDEN LEAVES

A bittersweet Czech tale. Betushka meets a fairy maiden, who dances all day with her, and gives her a basket of birch leaves, telling her not to look inside the basket before she returns home. She does, of course, and finds only leaves, which she mostly discards. When she returns, she finds the ones left in the basket are gold.

BLUEBEARD

A bloody tale, very influential for modern writers. A bride is brought to a castle and told not to enter a specific room. When she does, she finds all Bluebeard's previous brides there, slaughtered. She beats him through ingenuity.

CHILDE ROLAND AND BURD ELLEN

An enchanting fairy tale. Burd Ellen goes counterclockwise round a church to fetch a ball; she's taken by the King of Elfland, and Roland must enter into a quest to find her.

ECHO AND NARCISSUS

This tale is full of poignancy. Cursed by Juno, Echo can only echo what people say; her love for Narcissus, the beautiful boy, falls on deaf ears. Narcissus instead falls in love with a reflection of himself and turns into a flower.

GELERT THE FAITHFUL HOUND

A moving story about a Welsh prince, Llywelyn the Great, who returned home to find his baby gone and his dog covered in blood; in a rage, he slew the dog. The baby was found unharmed, a dead wolf beside it. The faithful dog was buried with honor.

HANS-MY-HEDGEHOG

I love this bonkers story from the Brothers Grimm, in which a half-boy/half-hedgehog is born to a father who is desperate for children. Disowned by his family, Hans wins over the princess and half the kingdom while riding on his pet rooster.

HERCULES AND CERBERUS

The final labor of the demi-god Hercules. In penance for killing his children, Hercules must perform 12 tasks. For this task, King Eurystheus sends him down to Hades to fetch the three-headed dog, Cerberus.

FURTHER READING

African

Beasts Made of Night by Tochi Onyebuchi

Akata Witch by Nnedi Okorafor

Black Leopard, Red Wolf by Marlon James

Children of Blood and Bone by Tomi Adeyemi

Arabian

Arabian Nights and Days by Naguib Mahfouz

Midnight's Children by Salman Rushdie

Sons of the Rumour by David Foster

The Wrath and the Dawn by Renée Ahdieh

One Thousand and One Nights by Hanan Al-Shaykh

1001 by Sanya Anwar

Greek

Memorial by Alice Oswald

Orfeia by Joanne Harris

Silence of the Girls by Pat Barker

The Hunger Games by Suzanne Collins

The Lost Books of the Odyssey by Zachary Mason

The Minotaur Takes A Cigarette Break by Steven Sherrill

Circe by Madeline Miller

Percy Jackson and the Olympians series by Rick Riordan

The Odyssey: A Modern Sequel by Nikos Kazantzakis

The Pelenopiad by Margaret Atwood

Ulysses by James Joyce

War Music by Christopher Logue

Irish

The Hound of Ulster by Rosemary Sutcliff

The Hounds of the Morrigan by Pat O'Shea

Japanese

Empress of all Seasons by Emiko Jean

Shadow of the Fox by Julie Kagawa

Flame in the Mist by Renée Ahdieh

King Arthur/Parthenia/Robin Hood

Arcadia by Iain Pears

Earthfasts by William Mayne

Here Lies Arthur by Philip Reeve

Robin Hood by Robert Muchamore

The Dark is Rising by Susan Cooper

The Once and Future King by T. H. White

Norse

American Gods by Neil Gaiman

Ragnarök: The End of the Gods by A. S. Byatt

The Gospel of Loki by Joanne Harris

Magnus Chase and the Gods of Asgard series by Rick Riordan

Russian

Old Peter's Russian Tales by Arthur Ransome

The Bear and the Nightingale by Katherine Arden

The Grisha trilogy by Leigh Bardugo

The House with Chicken Legs by Sophie Anderson

Vassa in the Night by Sarah Porter

Selkies

Rollrock Island by Margo Lanagan

The Blue Salt Road by Joanne M. Harris

Wild men/Bigfoots/Yetis

The Abominables by Eva Ibbotson

The Sasquatch Hunter's Almanac by Sharma Shields

ACKNOWLEDGMENTS

Charlene Fernandes, Kate Kirby, and Imogen Russell-Williams

HOW THE SUN WAS MADE

An Australian folktale, from the Dream Time, in which the Sun's birth is inspired by the cracking of an emu's egg and the yolk spilling out and lighting the world.

JACK AND THE BEANSTALK

A simple story about growing up and magic. A boy sells his cow for magic beans. They grow into an enormous beanstalk; he climbs up it and enters a land of giants, where he finds many riches, including a singing harp.

JACKAL OR TIGER?

A king and a queen in Hindustan quarrel over whether a sound is a jackal or a tiger. The queen is banished; her son grows up, and, after many adventures in which he is helped by a fairy, he and his mother are restored to his father. And the king never disagrees with his wife again.

SINBAD THE SAILOR

More from the Arabian Nights: The hero embarks on seven fantastical voyages, each one involving magical adventures, including rocs (giant birds), monsters, the Old Man of the Sea, and bird people.

THE BEE AND THE ORANGE TREE

Delightful 17th-century tale by Madame d'Aulnoy. A princess is shipwrecked and brought up by an ogress. Evading marriage to an ogre, she turns into a bee. There is a happy ending, don't worry.

THE COTTINGLEY FAIRIES

Two girls in the early 20th century tricked people into believing they'd photographed fairies. Explore how truth and fiction blend.

THE EMPTY POT

The dying Emperor of China decrees that any boy who wants to succeed him will receive a seed. Whoever gets the best results becomes Emperor. While all the other seeds grow, Jun's seed doesn't. He comes to the Emperor with an empty pot. But there's a surprise... Truth will out.

THE ENCHANTED WATCH

A French story with a nice spin on a common formula. A foolish younger son goes out into the world after his two brothers. With the help of a dog, cat, and snake, he wins a magic watch, which he uses to impress his father and win a princess. But the latter steals it. The princess ends up dead; the foolish son goes home.

THE LITTLE MERMAID

Hans Christian Andersen's wonderfully rich, sad tale about a young mermaid who falls for a human prince, and gives up her voice to be with him, only to be spurned for another.

THE REVENGE OF THE FORTY-SEVEN RŌNIN

A gripping Japanese legend, based on a historical event, in which 47 retainers avenge the death of their lord. This wonderful story brims with honor, glory, excitement, and pathos.

VIRGILIUS THE SORCEROR

This proves anything can make a fairy tale: this is about the real-life Roman poet Virgil. In the story, he becomes a magician who makes two copper dogs who bite some robbers to death. He then marries the daughter of the Sultan.